Home Office Solution

QUARRY

Home Office Solutions

Creating the Space That Works For You

LISA KANAREK

GLOUCESTER MASSACHUSETTS

QUARRY BOOKS

First published in the United States of America by
Quarry Books, an imprint of
Rockport Publishers, Inc.
33 Commercial Street
Gloucester, Massachusetts 01930-5089
Telephone: (978) 282-9590
Fax: (978) 283-2742

Library of Congress Cataloging-in-Publication data available

ISBN 1-59253-061-3

10 9 8 7 6 5 4 3 2

A portion of text for the Layered Lighting section is taken from
The Right Light (Rockport Publishers, 2000). Grateful
acknowledgment is made to the authors, Lisa Skolnik and Nora
Richter Greer.

Design: Cathy Kelley
Layout and Production: Walter Zekanoski and Sylvia Derichs
Front Cover Images: Tim Street-Porter (top); Tim Imrie/©Family
Circle/IPC Syndication (middle left); Wegner/Picture Press
(bottom)
Back Cover Images: IKEA
Illustrations: Madison Design and Advertising

Printed in Singapore

To my husband, Gary Weinstein, and our sons, Blake and Kyle.
Thank you for filling my life with laughter, love, and adventure.

Contents

Introduction: The One-Minute Commute

WHO NEEDS LONG COMMUTES, office gossip, and high overhead? Certainly not the 42 million people who call their home—or at least a portion of their home—their office. In fact, many new homes are being designed and built with a home office as part of the plan. Advances in technology, reduced equipment costs, and the removed stigma of working from home make home offices a perk for corporate employees (telecommuters) and a money and time-saver for entrepreneurs.

Working from home does present its share of challenges, however. While the benefits include minimal interruptions from others, no commute, and the ability to work at any hour, working from home requires equal parts of discipline and flexibility, not to mention organization. No one will be monitoring you to make sure you get the job done, and since you set your own hours, there's always a temptation to procrastinate—after all, you can always do the work later. The other side of the coin is that when you work at home, you never really get to leave your office. Balancing out family life, household chores, and working all within the confines of one house or apartment can be a challenge in itself.

That's why creating a comfortable and dedicated workspace is so important. It's imperative to separate your life from your work, and the first step toward that goal is to create a space in which you can work efficiently, effectively, and comfortably, away from the distractions of your everyday life. Stepping into your office, you should feel as though you've crossed an imaginary threshold:

you're at work now, away from the laundry, lawn, and cable TV. It's time to put on your mental work clothes—even if that means you're still wearing your pajamas.

Whether you're a full-time or part-time home-office professional, telecommuter, after-hours worker, or stay-at-home parent juggling a full household, your home office is a space in which you'll be spending a fair amount of time. So, it's important to think and plan ahead when designing your workspace. Whether your home office is located in a spare bedroom, finished basement, converted dining room, or den, you'll need to have just the right set-up, include the most up-to-date equipment, and be willing to think beyond the obvious. Deciding which room will make the ideal home office is the first step; deciding how to decorate,

furnish, and equip it follow. At every phase, proper planning will help make your work-at-home life easier. From picking out a desk to storing your pencils, from deciding just what computer configuration is best for you to picking that perfect shade of color for the walls, every decision you make when you set up and decorate your home office will have an effect on your productivity and your morale. This book will help you plan your space to maximize comfort, creativity, and efficiency, and show you just how great working at home can be.

So put away your business suit (if you don't have any appointments today), pour a cup of coffee, and learn how to create a home office that is not only functional, but a space that will be the envy of your corporate counterparts.

How to Make a Better Business at Home
Home Office Planning, Set-up, and Organization

Running a successful business at home means taking the skills, sense, and habits you've developed over the years and putting them to work outside of the traditional office environment. While the tasks you'll be handling might not differ all that much from your old suit-and-tie job, your surroundings will have changed immensely. No more traffic jams or long, crowded commutes, no boss breathing down your neck if you're a few minutes late, no huge dry-cleaning bills, ties, or high heels. But gone too is the unlimited supply of paper and supplies, the friendly mailroom workers who take care of packing, shipping, the cleaning staff who take care of vacuuming your space and taking out your garbage and recycling. You'll also be away from the camaraderie of office

life: no more friendly water-cooler conversation, peer pressure to perform, or easygoing lunch hour excursions.

Yes, the work-at-home life can be a major adjustment, but many find that adjustment easier by creating sensible home offices that are comfortable, functional, and that address the specific challenges of working at home. In this section, you'll learn how to plan and design a space that will allow you to work with as much or even more focus, creativity, and productivity as you did in the corporate world, with the comforting advantages that only working at home can provide.

The Home Worker

THE DECISION TO WORK AT HOME seems like an easy one. No more commuting, getting dressed for work, or buying expensive lunches; now you can be your own boss; make your own decisions; work when you want on what you want. But in reality, working at home presents unique challenges and situations, and it's not for everyone. There are substantial expenses involved in setting up a successful home-based business, and without a steady paycheck, that can be risky. And many people find the telecommuting lifestyle lonely and isolated, and miss the day-to-day contact they once shared with their fellow workers and commuters.

Before deciding to work at home, it's important to determine whether or not the lifestyle suits you. Consider the financial risks and rewards, as well as the social ones. And thoroughly evaluate your own unique work quirks and create a home office and a routine that works for you.

Identifying Your Needs

Of course, not every home office is the same, nor should it be. Different types of businesses demand different kinds of offices, whether they are located in corporate parks or in a home. Think about the kind of business you'll be conducting, and then decide what kind of home office you'll need.

The Telecommuter

Staying on the company payroll, but working from home rather than the corporate office can offer the best of both worlds.

Continuing to work with your familiar colleagues and on familiar projects—not to mention continuing to earn a regular paycheck—makes the adjustment to home office life easy. And often, the corporation provides all or some of the equipment needed to set up, so you don't need to spend huge amounts of money to get up and running at home. Your office can be purely utilitarian—you'll probably still have all your meetings at the corporate office—or as cozy and charming as you wish it to be.

Opposite **Sharing a home office makes sense because you can cut expenses by sharing a communal file, copier, and storage area. The workstations don't have to be exactly the same, as shown in this shared office where one station features unusual artwork and collectibles, while the other has a simple, yet functional, look.**

DID YOU KNOW?

The average office worker receives 201 phone, paper, and e-mail messages a day.
— *Real Simple* magazine

Each American uses an average of 749 pounds of paper products each year (around 187 billion pounds of paper for the entire United States).
— *Quill Pen Pal* publication

The average U.S. adult Internet user will spend 9.5 months reading e-mail over the course of his/her life.
— *Office Solutions* magazine

U.S. workers spend one-third of their time at a computer, and 80 percent believe technology has made their job easier.
— **John J. Heldrich Center at Rutgers University**

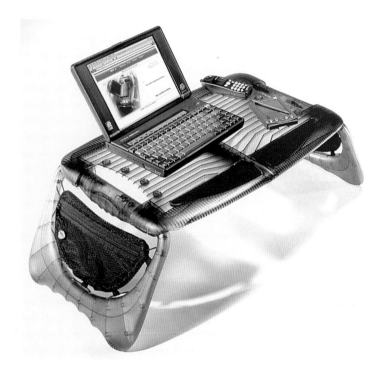

Above **The Lap-station's ingenious design turns any room into a functional, part-time office. Shock-absorbing rubber feet offer a stable work surface, and built-in wrist pads help minimize injury.**

Below **Working from home means you can ditch the corporate look and create an office that matches your personal style. This inviting office caters to both the creative and task-minded home office professional. Smooth lines, natural wood, and an area rug in muted colors create a soothing, calming, and inspirational environment.**

WORKING THE WAY YOU WORK

The beauty of a home office is that it can reflect your personality and the way you work. If you enjoy working early in the morning when the light hits your office just right, make sure you arrange your office to capture every ray of sunlight. If you prefer to work on a sofa instead of a computer workstation or desk, furnish your office with a comfortable couch, or chair and ottoman, and pull up a lap table to hold your notebook computer while you work.

The Home Business

Whether you are selling real estate or starting your own Web-design firm, launching a home-based business presents special challenges. In addition to the capital you need to get your business rolling—for equipment, marketing, possibly even staff—you'll need to create a space that is professional looking to entertain clients.

The Freelancer

If you have a marketable skill—as a writer, artist, or business consultant, for example—making yourself available as a hired gun working out of your home can be profitable and exciting. You'll need to develop a space that suits your needs: an architect might have meetings onsite but will still require a large in-home studio to do his or her work. On the other hand, a financial analyst who does most of his work onsite might get away with just a "portable office": a briefcase, cell phone, and a laptop computer.

The Part-Time Office

For those who work onsite part of the week and at home for the remainder, setting up the home office presents special challenges. You might not be willing to devote an entire room to an office that will only be used one or two days a week; or, you might find that pulling up stakes at the end of each workday and packing up all your projects can be stressful and confusing. Laptop computers make things easier, as do good, portable organizers or a personal digital assistant.

The Shared Office

If the cost of running your business alone is too much, or if you are just lonely for a little human contact during the day, consider a shared home office. If you have a large room, lease out half the space to a colleague or to anyone else who needs a home office but lacks the space in which to create one. In addition to the money you'll earn by renting the space, you can defray some of the costs of business for both of you by sharing a printer, office supplies purchased in bulk, and a fax machine. Of course, the shared office presents special challenges—whether you share it with a renter, partner, or even your spouse. You'll need to design an office space that clearly divides work areas and minimizes distraction.

ORGANIZING YOUR BRIEFCASE

For those who work at home as well as onsite, a briefcase (or backpack, or tote bag) that works as a portable office is essential. Use file folders as portable in-boxes. A small stash of office supplies (pens, a small stapler, paper clips, rubber bands, note cards, envelopes, and stamps) can be stored in an inside pocket, a pencil case, or clear zippered bag. A decent organizer—either a notebook or a hand-held personal digital assistant—keeps vital information like phone numbers, to-do lists, and your calendar at your fingertips.

The Work-at-Home Parent

One of the most common reasons for working at home is in order to spend more time with your family. Men and women alike see working at home as the ideal situation, keeping them in close proximity to their children while they continue their careers. But of course, working with kids at home—no matter what their ages—presents special challenges. Young children will not be satisfied to leave you alone and may demand attention when you're trying to work; indeed, parents who think they've seen the end of day-care costs are often surprised to find that they still need to leave their babies and pre-schoolers with sitters for at least part of the day.

The "Home" Office—Spaces for Running the Household

Not every home office is designed to run a business: running a household is a full-time job in itself and can be as much work—if not more work—as running a small business. The household manager has no set hours. There's no shutting your door, turning off the phone, and delaying problems until the morning. With that much work and responsibility comes the need for a place to keep everyone on track—an organization center, where you can pay bills, collect school forms from your children, maintain a family calendar, and store any paperwork that has to deal with your family.

An organization center doesn't require an elaborate set up. The basics include some type of planning system, whether paper-based, handheld, or computerized; a desk, computer workstation, or built-in work area, and a computer and printer as necessary. Your family organization center (FOC) can be set up in the corner of your kitchen, within an armoire in your den, or tucked in a roll-top desk in your bedroom. Even if you run a business out of your home, set up an FOC in another part of your home (especially if you want to take a home office tax deduction). Or, you can set one up within your home office, designated by a separate workstation. Wherever you decide to set up your center, make it a rule that any family-related papers go straight to the FOC, rather than get strewn about your home.

An FOC is a better alternative to a kitchen counter overflowing with bills, permission slips, and school menus. Many of the papers you receive from your child's school are time sensitive, meaning that something left in a pile for more than a week could mean your child misses a field trip, after-school activity, or friend's birthday party. If your family organization center is located in your kitchen, keep your files accessible, yet out of the way of prying hands and eyes. Ideally, files should be stored in a drawer equipped with a hanging file rack or cabinet with a pullout file rack. A sturdy, two-drawer file cabinet should be enough to hold most, if not all, of your family's files. If you can't find a place for your file cabinet in your kitchen, look for space in a nearby closet, or keep the cabinet in your kitchen with a tablecloth draped over it. It could double as a place to hold your cookbooks on top.

Multitasking is all the rage lately, so why not be creative about where you set up your FOC. The kitchen is a great place as you can easily shift from paying bills to food preparation, but what about other areas in your home? For example, you might set up your FOC in the laundry room, along with a phone line and plenty of outlets. This will make it easy to throw in a load of laundry while working at your desk—and there's no chance of missing the buzzer on your dryer.

Opposite A suspended desktop with shelves above and below keeps the bouncing ball type focused. With everything within reach, including magazines, the bouncing ball does not need to leave the desk every few minutes and risk getting distracted by another project.

Working With the Way You Work

One of the keys to working at home is getting in touch with your own personal working style and learning to accommodate it. If you're easily distracted, for example, you'll need to create a workspace that keeps distractions to a minimum. If you know that you need absolute and total quiet in order to concentrate, you'll need to create a space that is as far removed as possible from the comings and goings of your family, pets, and even your neighbors. Acknowledging your bad work habits and accentuating your good ones is essential before you set up your office. Whether you're the type of person who likes to flit from project to project or you're one of those who likes to tackle one at a time, you can design a space that actually will help you become more effective and make your office more functional.

It's much easier to embrace your style than it is to pretend to be someone you're not. Don't model yourself after an associate, your spouse, or anyone else. Everyone works, organizes, and functions differently, so what works for one person might not work for another. Understanding your natural work style can mean the difference between working in a beautifully decorated space where you can't concentrate or find what you need, and working in a well-designed office where you feel comfortable and can be productive.

The Bouncing Ball

Are you the type of person who bounces from project to project, without completing a single one? If so, you could be a *bouncing ball*. A bouncing ball wants to accomplish everything, yet has trouble doing one thing at a time. To get more focused, set up your office to feature as little distractions as possible. Try situating your main workstation in a corner, with your back to the room. Keep the walls you face free from schedules, task lists, anything that suggests that other projects need your immediate attention. Instead, hang a soothing photo or painting

EVALUATING YOUR WORK STYLE

Not sure just how you work? Do you get to the end of the day without a clear sense of what you've accomplished? Get a better sense of your work style and productivity by doing a little self-evaluation experiment. Every day for the next week, keep your daily planner open on your desk (or use a legal pad or your computer), and set an alarm clock or timer to go off every hour. When it does, stop what you're doing briefly, and jot down the time and what you've done in the past hour. At the end of the day, take a look at what you've done, and how you've done it. Did you focus on one task for most of the day? Or did you go from project to project? After a week or so, you'll not only get a better sense of your work style but also be able to more accurately estimate the amount of time you'll need to devote to certain projects and tasks, which will make planning future projects easier.

in your line of sight, or—if you don't think it will distract you—place your desk in front of a window.

Most any layout configuration will work for the bouncing-ball style, just so long as you keep materials for other projects out of easy reach. While sitting at your chair, make a work circle by spreading out your arms on either side to see how far you can comfortably reach, and marking these points. The same goes for what you can see in your peripheral vision. Don't put anything work-related other than your basic tools (tape dispenser or pen holder, etc.) in that area. Keep in boxes, magazine holders, and the like out of sight—and out of mind, at least until you finish what you're doing.

Use stacking bins that sit next to your workstation and label them "to do," "to file," and "to read," to deal with your projects as well as incoming papers and other materials that need to be processed regularly. Or, single out a bookshelf to hold certain projects. Place stacking trays on the shelves labeled "future projects," "urgent," "drop-dead urgent," and so on. The top of a bookshelf is ideal for a plant, artificial flower arrangement or decorative items that won't get in your way.

How do you keep all your projects straight if you're not constantly looking at them? Try keeping one daily or weekly to-do list and refer to it often. It can be a list within a spiral note-book, hand-held organizer, or computerized planning program. Pay attention to this list. Determine which tasks have a higher priority and concentrate on accomplishing those tasks first.

The best rule of thumb for the bouncing ball is to *keep it simple*. The less you have in your office, the less you'll be distracted and instead, able to focus on the task at hand.

The Collector

Do you keep things "just in case" or because you think you "might need them someday?" Is your home stacked with out-of-date magazines, newspapers, and mail that you didn't quite find the time to open? Face it: You're a collector. Aside from the incessant clutter, which is not easy on the eyes, being a collector can lead to professional disasters when you need something and you can't find it under all your paper piles.

The best home office setup for controlling the tendency to keep anything and everything is one that won't allow you to do so. How can you accomplish this? Opt for a setup with the bare minimum of surfaces on which to put things. Nothing attracts the collector's clutter better than a clean, unused surface. Think about what you do during the day. How much room do you need to spread out? Will a computer workstation and small table suffice for work surfaces in your home office? Perhaps another small table itself is adequate to hold your phone, fax, or other necessary piece of equipment.

Drawers can pose another problem for collectors. The more drawers you have, the more places to stash unnecessary items. A few drawers never hurt anyone and add to the functionality of a desk or computer workstation, but limit the number of drawers in your office to four. Likewise, be wary of decorative hideaway storage units that can hide clutter for you. You might be tempted to stuff papers in here without dealing with them. While out of sight, out of mind, may be an effective way to get one task accomplished at a time, it's not great when you have bills piling up behind the doors of an aesthetically pleasing French country-style armoire in your home office.

Of course, paper is not the only culprit. Take a look at your office and think about what's there. Do you use everything you see every day? Look at each thing you're holding on to. Ask yourself if it serves a specific purpose. And if it does, how often is it called upon? If you don't use it at all, get rid of it. If you don't use it that often, mark it as one of those pieces you can tuck away in a closet or storage unit.

Do yourself a favor and establish a system for going through papers once a week—but not less than every two weeks. Do you have stacks of magazines in your office that you have not referred to in months? If so, block out a morning—or a day, depending on how much you have—to go through the stack and see if there's anything worth keeping. If you don't have time to read everything, tear out articles that look interesting and put these in a file for looking at when you do have the time (in between appointments or while traveling). Think of all the room you'll be saving if you only clip one or two articles—if that—from each magazine. For periodicals that you don't need on a regular basis but simply cannot part with, organize them into boxes clearly labeled with the name of the publication and the year, and store them somewhere they won't get in the way. And set a limit for the number of boxes you'll keep; when you add a new box, make it a point to throw out the oldest one.

A similar approach can make your files more manageable. At the end of each project, weed out all the extraneous correspondence and paperwork from the project file, and move them into a separate archive. Box up old files every few months or years—depending on the number of files—and set up an archive in your basement, attic, or in the back of a closet. Most importantly, put a moratorium on archived files—say three years—and make it a point to purge your archive on an annual basis. Make sure you store the boxes on pallets or shelves to avoid potential water damage.

miss deadlines, and sometimes put more work into a project than a client expected or is willing to pay for.

Fear not. There are ways to help a perfectionist set more realistic goals without compromising his or her own standards. Unlike the bouncing-ball type, you could probably use a few distractions—but just enough to help you relax and put your tasks in perspective. Keep reminders around your office to help you stay on top of your priorities without losing track of them. Photos of your loved ones above your desk will remind you that there comes a time to close up shop and go home, even if home is only upstairs. A whiteboard with each of your projects listed—along with the deadline and a budget for how much time (and money) should be spent on it—will help you stay on top of your work, rather then buried beneath it. And finally, an attractive, comfortable chair that will invite you to take an occasional break and put your feet up could be just the thing you need. Try scheduling a regular afternoon phone call, tea break, or even a half hour to watch the news—to help you step back from your projects for a little while.

The Lookout

The *lookout* follows the out-of-sight, out-of-mind philosophy and fears putting anything away. She keeps files stacked on her desk, office supplies on open shelves, and reference books on the floor instead of behind cabinet doors. She regularly tosses what she does not need, but she never puts anything out of sight, knowing full well that if she does, she'll never return to it. The lookout knows that what's out of sight is out of mind and needs to keep everything right in front of her.

While the lookout's work style isn't in itself a problem, it can be an aesthetic nightmare. Open shelves filled with boxes of office supplies, reams of paper stacked on the floor, and stacks of files might be efficient, but they're not so pretty to

Above A perfectionist's home office, with its neatly organized shelves and every-thing-in-its-place look, is tidy, yet not boring. A decorative vase and checkerboard rug bring color, texture, and balance to a potentially stark office.

The Perfectionist

A *perfectionist* often confuses perfectionism with organization. While appearing organized on the surface, the perfectionist's quest for perfection might actually be hampering his or her business. There is nothing wrong with striving for perfection (or near perfection)—except when your quest for perfection affects the quantity of the work you produce and your efficiency. Are you obsessed with every last detail, to the point that you are continually missing deadlines? Are you spending so much time on projects that your family has forgotten what you look like and your clients are wondering why you billed for thirty hours on a project that should have only taken fifteen? Perfectionists often concentrate too much on the minutia of their work, at the expense of the big picture: they lose track of time,

Left The lookout suffers from the fear of "out of sight, out of mind." One way to alleviate that fear is to use large, open shelves and wall organizers. The red cabinet below the desk takes the place of desk drawers. For maximum effectiveness, be sure to label each drawer with its contents.

look at. But if you're a lookout, you don't have to change your workstyle for the sake of design.

When choosing a desk, select one with a minimal amount of drawers—you can keep the office supplies you use daily or weekly on top of your desk in a desktop organizer—and enough room to spread out your papers. A U-shaped workstation setup (see Designing Your Office) is ideal for the lookout, who needs lots of surface space within arm's reach. Add a hutch to your desk to store supplies, reference materials, and even memorabilia without sacrificing valuable desktop real estate. Invest in wicker baskets or metal or plastic bins to hold each project. Clearly labeled, they can be pulled

out and left on the desk when you're working and stowed (still in sight) on open bookshelves when you're not. Another option is stacking bins that don't need to be moved while you're working.

Instead of covering your office walls with framed photographs, paintings, or memorabilia, convert one wall into a giant bulletin board by adding corkboard (with protective padding on the back to avoid damaging or staining the wall). You could use the board to hold anything from postcards to schedules, and have information at your fingertips instead of tucked away in a drawer— where you'll probably forget it!

The Do-It-All

While working at home often means doing everything yourself, there are some times when it's necessary to delegate projects. But some people never have and never will feel comfortable delegating. These *do-it-alls* take responsibility for many more tasks than they should: while someone else could handle routine sales calls, the assembly of marketing packets, and the layout of the company newsletter, for example, the do-it-all takes responsibility for everything. While the do-it-all might see herself as the ideal, all-in-one worker, she frequently oversteps boundaries by doing others' work for them, or wastes time attending tasks that could be handled by someone else. If you're a market analyst hired to create a survey and analyze the results, for example, it's important to concentrate on those tasks, and let someone else worry about stuffing the envelopes and tallying up the responses.

But the do-it-all can be reformed. If you're a do-it-all, learn to give up control. By convincing yourself that others are capable of handling various tasks, you can devote more energy to tasks that only you can and should handle. Learn to outsource certain tasks: hire quality people and learn to manage them. If you follow up on their progress, without looking over their shoulder every minute, you'll find that others are capable of being effective helpers, and that you are able to devote more time, energy, and creativity to the more important aspects of your job.

The Procrastinator

Many great minds acknowledge that procrastination is indeed an art. The *procrastinator* can delay working for any number of reasons, from unopened mail to unmade beds. A procrastinator might put off making a decision for fear of making the wrong one or put off beginning a project until they have every last bit of relevant information.

For those working at home, procrastination can be extremely dangerous. The problem with the home office is that you never really leave it, so you feel as though you can always do something later. Procrastinators must think carefully when designing their home office. They should locate their office as far away from the main area of the house as possible—guest houses, basements, and attics are excellent locations—and make it a point to start work at a set time every day. By keeping their work lives and their home lives separate and maintaining a regular schedule, procrastinators can force themselves to keep moving and stay on top of all their tasks—from office work to housework.

THE PAPER CHASE

Whether you're a collector or just paranoid, getting rid of paper can be difficult for lots of people. Some fear that they'll need the information again; others fear that throwing away papers that include sensitive personal information—Social Security number, financial information, credit card numbers, and the like—are vulnerable to identity theft. To avoid paper pile up, invest in a paper shredder and set it with the recycling bin right near the spot where you read your mail. Ditch every piece of paper as soon as it's been read and determined unimportant.

AFTER deciding where your home office will be but before you buy furniture and furnishings, you will need to get the room ready. The FREEDOM (as in freedom from corporate life) plan will get you started on the right track.

Home Office Plan

Find the right place for your office. After carefully considering the factors that determine the ideal place for a home office, decide where your home office will be located.

Remove nonbusiness-related items. Sports equipment, clothing, and any other personal items belong in another part of your home, especially if you plan to claim the home-office deduction on your income tax form.

Envision a workable arrangement. Where should your desk and computer workstation go? Make sure you have enough room for existing furniture, equipment, and supplies or items you know you'll be adding to your home office later.

Establish home office workstations. Mentally break your home office down into various parts. One workstation may be your printing station with your printer, paper, and extra ink cartridges. Another area could be your drafting station with a drafting table and movable storage cart.

Dump, sort, and store items. This is your chance to declutter. Toss or donate what you don't need and use boxes to store what you know you will use when your office is set up, or put items away as you sort.

Organize like items. It's easier to find what you need if you store similar items together. All of your extra office supplies should be stored in one place and your computer manuals in another. You'll limit the number of places you have to look when you need to find something.

Maintain your office. Once your office is set up and organized, it's up to you to maintain the space you have created. If you spend only fifteen minutes putting files away, updating your to-do list, and planning for the next day, you'll save four times that the next day.

Carving Out a Space

THE FIRST STEP to establishing a successful home-based business is to find the ideal location in
your home to set up shop. Here, creativity is key: You need to recognize wasted and underused
space, and visualize new uses for it. Think outside the box: Your dream office might be a spacious
attic or a compact but functional former walk-in closet. Walk through your home with notebook

and pen in hand and view it as though through the eyes of someone seeing it for the first time. Take a would-this-space-work? approach to each area of your home. Look at every corner, closet, and any other area of your home that at first glance may seem useless. Don't forget about laundry rooms and wet bars. As you go through, list the good points and bad points of each space you look at: consider the natural light, the availability of electrical outlets and phone jacks, the proximity to high-traffic areas of your home that might distract you from your work. If the good points outweigh the bad, give that space serious consideration. Sometimes the spaces you thought you'd never use are the ones with the greatest potential.

If you've lived in the same home for years and think you've exhausted every possible space that could be used for a home office, think again. What about the space under your staircase? There may be just enough room there for a computer workstation and two-drawer file cabinet. Consider putting an unused, upstairs landing or alcove to work: if the traffic through that area is limited, capture that space for your home office.

Once you've identified a space (or spaces) in your home that would work as a home office, start weighing the options. Keep in mind that the space you choose must be comfortable and conducive to working. The perfect space should be quiet enough that environmental noise—be it street traffic, the neighbor's dog, or your kids playing video games in the next room—won't distract you from your work, or be audible during phone calls with clients or colleagues. Also consider whether the room will be comfortable to work in. Is it too hot in the summer and an igloo in the winter? And consider the

availability of natural light; just like working onsite, you should vie for an office with a sunny window to lift your spirits and energize you. So before you entirely commit to using a particular space for a home office, give the spot a test-drive: set up your computer and other equipment in that area, have the files you need on hand, and try working there for one full month. If after that time you find that you enjoy working in that space and have stopped escaping to the kitchen, den, or bedroom to work most of the time, then you've found the place to call home office.

The size of your home office matters less than the function. A large home office is not necessarily more functional than a small, well-designed home office. More square footage means you'll have more space to spread out your equipment, files, and reference materials. But if your printer, fax, and vital files aren't properly situated, you'll waste countless hours each day just jumping up and down and moving around to reach what you need. On the other hand, a small, cramped home office with barely enough room to squeeze in a chair, computer stand, and file cabinet will be an uncomfortable place to work and may even mean that you'll have to enlist other rooms for supplies, reference materials, and files.

If you've been working out of the same home office for many years, it's probably a good time to reevaluate your current space. You may find another, more functional space in your home for your office. Remember, as your business grows, so will your office needs. A home office choice doesn't mean a lifetime commitment. You can change the place you choose as your home office as often as you change careers or businesses.

Opposite **No space is out of bounds for a home office. With only a small amount of space under the stairs, there is enough room for a sideboard and desk. The built-in shelves in the next room offer sufficient storage for reference materials.**

Top Spots for a Home Office

While a home office can be located just about anywhere, the ideal spot offers not only room to set up, but a clear division between your work-space and the rest of your home. Situating your workspace in a separate room, a separate floor, or even a separate structure is a great way to keep work from overflowing into your home life, and vice versa. For those whose homes have room to spare, here are some of the ideal spaces to consider for a home office.

A Spare Bedroom

A spare bedroom is the first place to consider for a home office. Generally, spare bedrooms have enough room for a desk, computer work-station, bookcase, and a few file cabinets. A key source of storage will be the closet, making it easier to keep all of your supplies, reference materials, and samples (if you represent a product or products)

in one place. The advan-tage of a spare bed-room is that you can use it exclusively for business (a nice tax advantage) and you won't ever have to dismantle your office or hide important files because you'll be the only one using the room. Also, you can furnish and decorate it to reflect your moods and interests.

A Guest Bedroom

Like the spare bedroom, a guest bedroom makes for a great home office, but this situation may pose a few problems if you want to continue to have the space available to overnight guests. The first is square footage. Add a desk and computer workstation to a guest bedroom and you'll probably be left with little space to work, as the bed and chest of drawers you already have in the room will be taking up most of the space. Try moving the dresser into the closet (if possible) and replace the large bed with a foldout couch or pull-down (Murphy) bed.

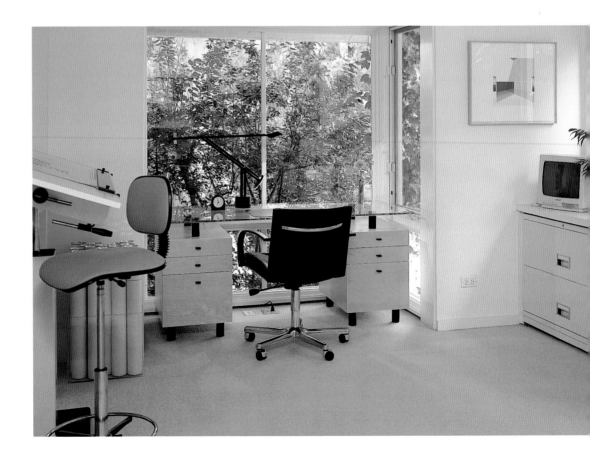

Basement

Do you have a basement that you're only using for storage and perhaps laundry? The right basement can be transformed into a fully functioning, thriving home office. A key advantage to a basement is space. Since the basement usually is the size of the floor above it, carving out enough space for your equipment and furniture should not be difficult. However, you may run into problems if your basement is damp or has a tendency to flood, is not well lit—even window-less—or is cold and sterile. While the last two of these variables can be easily remedied, the first cannot. Don't take unnecessary chances with your valuable papers and equipment. Even if your basement only floods occasionally, look for another spot.

To create a workable, desirable, and functional home office in your basement, paint the walls in bright colors, like yellow, light blue, or white to keep the space from looking dreary. Add plenty of task lighting to brighten the space and to provide the light you need to work. White melamine or light oak furniture will give your basement home office a lighter feel. If you don't want to go to the expense of installing wall-to-wall carpeting, be sure that your basement home office configuration includes at least an area rug or two to soften and warm up the space.

Converted Garage

Sure, it's filled with junk right now, but that's all the more proof that you really don't need the space to store your car. If your garage is underused and space inside the house is at a premium, you might consider converting all or part of it into a functional home office. Talk to a contractor about renovating the space; you might put up a wall and split the area into two separate rooms, one a heated, cozy home office, and the other a storage shed for everything from rakes to shovels to storage of old files.

Right **A triangular desk with a back-splash that doubles as a headboard makes use of a tight space without looking cramped. Reference materials, supplies, and a place for a "power nap" are only inches away.**

Below **The wall-to-ceiling shelves along the back wall of this counter arrangement office store less-frequently used supplies. The two adjustable lamps serve both the office and sleeping areas.**

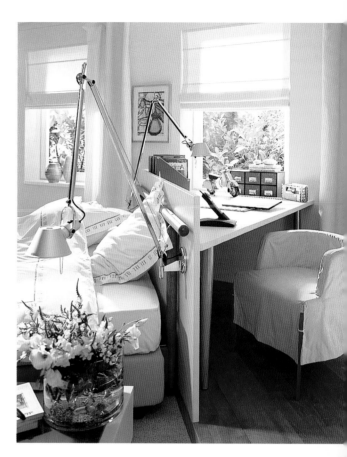

Attic

Most people think of an attic as being a dark, musty, unlit space with low ceilings. But with the right planning, most attics can be transformed into desirable home offices. You may raise the roof, add a windowed dormer, or reconfigure the beams to be less obtrusive. Adding one or two skylights will brighten an attic home office, especially if it has limited windows. Even if parts of your attic seem useless, be creative: the crawlspace beneath the eaves makes great out-of-the-way storage for seldom-used or archived files, and open bookshelves can serve double duty as both storage units and room dividers. Before you decide to convert your attic into a home office, have a reputable contractor look at the space and give you a quote. There are various factors that you may not anticipate with an attic conversion, including the need to move pipes and build stairs to the attic if they don't exist already. Also, ask your contractor to inspect your floor joists to ensure they will support the weight of one or more adults. Most ceiling joists are 2 inches (5 cm) X 6 inches (15.25 cm) or 2 inches (5 cm) X 8 inches (20.30 cm), but need to be 2 inches (5 cm) X 12 inches (30.50 cm) to provide enough support.

Guest Quarters

A detached home office offers several advantages over a traditional spare-bedroom home office. The first is privacy: It takes more effort for a family member to interrupt you than if your office is inside your home. Another advantage is the ability to entertain clients without asking them to traipse through your home. For anyone who has ever had to do a massive cleanup before a client meeting, this cleaning reprieve is welcome. To minimize the number of times you need to go back to your home during the day, furnish your office with a coffeepot or electric tea kettle, a microwave, small refrigerator, and a few dishes and utensils. Install an intercom system to stay in contact with your family, and to be available to receive deliveries or guests who might mistakenly choose the wrong door. If the home you purchased or built doesn't have a detached structure, you can order a prefab home office that is delivered and constructed within a few days, or hire a contractor to build a small home office for you. Before you do anything, check with your city to make sure you can add another structure to your property. And be sure to install proper security on the structure, and invest in insurance, to protect any expensive equipment or supplies you'll be leaving there.

Left Whether your space is large or small, organize essential supplies in decorative boxes and baskets and keep these close to your main workstation. This will optimize the functionality of your workstation while making it look good at the same time.

Bottom left A small, detached cabin can serve as a home office or guest quarters. The bright blue exterior and lime green shades give the office the whimsical look of a dollhouse.

Bottom right Inside, a tiny but efficient workspace features enough adequate desk space and wall-storage space. Adding a compact refrigerator would eliminate the need to leave the cabin for refreshments.

Underused Spaces

You may not have an entire room to spare, but if you take a look at your home and the way that you use it, you might realize that there are rooms that are not really living up to their potential. Think about places where you simply don't spend any time: the formal dining room that you never really use or the living room that you only go into when you have to dust the furniture. Why not put those rooms to work?

Living Room

Some people's living rooms are like museums—the only things missing are the stanchions and velvet rope to keep children and anyone else who might touch anything from doing so. But even if you have a very formal living room, you might still put it to use as an office rather than waste an often-large room that is rarely used anyway. You don't have to part with the formal air of the space. Simply take advantage of furniture that is beautiful to look at and will cleverly conceal your equipment. Many armoires manufactured these days have been designed for home office use. They are functional in that they give your office materials a place to live and they also blend in well with most living rooms. If the living room is the first room people see when walking into your home, install swinging wooden doors, French doors, or a pocket door to keep your home office private. You can still maintain privacy yet let light into your home office by choosing doors with divided lights (separate panes of glass).

Left **Combining a home office with a living room within a loft underscores the need for organization. The nearby television stand provides office supply storage.**

Dining Room

How often do you entertain guests? Once a year or twice a year—if that often? And when you entertain, do you use your dining room? Chances are, your formal dining room goes unused most of the year. Instead of wasting this perfectly functional room, put it to use as your home office. You can completely transform the room by replacing the chandelier with a ceiling fan and the dining room table with an ergonomically correct computer workstation, or you can move in the equipment you need on a workstation on casters. When the holidays roll around, simply wheel your workstation into another room. Use the furniture you already have in the space. Turn your buffet into an office-supply cabinet. Sound crazy? Only if you entertain often. Perhaps your dining room is unfurnished right now—and will be for a couple more years due to a lack of time and money. What more perfect opportunity could there be for your home office?

THERE ARE a few factors to consider before using a particular room for your office. As you evaluate the areas of your home for your selection, keep the following in mind:

Home Office Location Checklist

- **Will you feel comfortable working in the space?** A beautifully designed home office that's located far from your family, including in the basement, may be attractive and functional, but if you don't enjoy working there, you're wasting space that could be used for something else.

- **Is there enough space to work effectively?** Your office will have to be big enough to accommodate at least a desk and file cabinet. It doesn't have to be enormous, but it should be big enough for office basics—and be spacious enough for you to move around in comfortably.

- **Will you be able to concentrate in the space?** The number of distractions you will face on a regular basis is important. Your challenge will be to keep them to a minimum. Your family, the television, and refrigerator located too close to your home office, will seriously hinder your productivity. Also, be sure your space is essentially soundproof. If you're planning to make phone calls from your home office, barking dogs, your washer and dryer, and children playing in another room will not make a professional impression.

- **Is the space adequately lit—and if not, can that be easily remedied?** Lighting is a vital part of any home office setup. Poor lighting causes eyestrain, fatigue, and irritability. Make sure you will be able to add adequate lighting, especially if this space has only one window.

- **Can the space accommodate your electrical needs?** It's vital that you have a good power source to run your equipment. Check with an electrician to make sure your chosen space will have enough power to keep everything running.

- **Can the space accommodate a phone line?** A business without a phone is like a car without gas, so be sure you can set up adequate phone lines for phone, fax, and Internet access in your chosen space.

- **Can you make permanent changes to the configuration of the space?** While most of the changes you make won't affect the sale price of your home, be sure to consider the ones that will. If you have a three-bedroom home and you decide to knock down a wall to create two bedrooms—the larger of which you plan to use for your home office—you will significantly affect the resale value of your home.

- **Whichever space you decide to turn into a home office, think long term.** It's better to invest in the right location up front than to settle for a space that costs less but will no longer suit your needs in a year or two.

Right A converted
dining room, with a
solid-wood table
used in place of a
traditional desk,
blends modern equip-
ment with exquisite
antiques. The in box
keeps incoming mail
in one place, while
the wicker basket
below stores magazines
for easy reference.

Last Resorts

Just as there are prime spots for setting up your office, there are others that should only be considered when all else fails.

The Bedroom

Bedrooms should be for sleeping—period. When you mix bedrooms with business, you're asking for sleepless nights, added pressures, and no distinction between your work and personal life. When your office is in your bedroom, you're essentially sleeping with your job. If you've had a bad day, the experiences and emotions of that day follow you to bed. Unless you can physically block out your workspace from your bedroom using Japanese screens, a partial wall made out of glass blocks or open bookshelves, or even a simple curtain, find another place to set up shop. If your bedroom is your only option for setting

up a home office and your space is limited (no sitting area in sight), go for a compact set up. An armoire; roll-top computer workstation; or a small, ergonomically correct desk with enough room to hold a laptop will occupy little space. Be sure to find a desk with enough file drawers and space for supplies you use regularly. At the end of your workday, literally close your office and ignore it until the morning.

The Kitchen

Using the kitchen as a home office isn't as bad as using your bedroom, but it's still not the optimum work environment. Unless you live alone, your kitchen office may be as noisy and crowed as a downtown street. Having to constantly move papers and files to make room for daily meals or snacks is a waste of time and energy, not to mention the perfect way to lose important information. If you have to use part

Above Although this office is situated in a large kitchen, everything related to the office is in one area. The supplies stored within the wooden cabinet in the corner are organized by type of item. The huge window offers plenty of natural light and an interesting view.

Top **Floor-to-ceiling open shelves provide enough room in this small closet for storage and equipment. An articulating keyboard pushes out of the way when not being used, and the window ledge provides an additional work and storage area. Frequently used letterhead, paper, and reference books are stored vertically to save space.**

Bottom **Supplies tucked in labeled wooden boxes, a shelf for a laptop, and a chair that fits perfectly behind closed doors make this closet office functional and compact.**

Opposite **A walk-in closet, retrofitted with shelves of varying sizes, houses a fully functional home office that doesn't interfere with the owner's personal life during nonbusiness hours. The chair, stored outside of the closet when not in use, blends in beautifully with the rest of the room.**

of your kitchen as a home office, do your best to capture a cabinet or corner that is used only for business and used only by you. Ideally, put your desk behind cabinets (flat or roll-down) or wooden doors (accordion or two-panel).

Creative Home Office Spaces

Of course, you don't have to resort to setting up your office in your kitchen just because you don't have a spare bedroom. Take a good look at your home and let your imagination run wild. Great, hardworking offices can be set up in the most unusual of spaces, if you think outside the box and get creative.

Walk-in Closet

The claustrophobia-prone may not do well in a closet, but if you don't mind narrow, closed spaces, a walk-in closet might be just what the home office planner ordered. With a few mirrors, a small, cramped closet can be transformed into a functional home office as the mirror reflects light and will make the space seem twice the size. Line the walls with shelves if they are not already in place. Install wall-to-wall counters to hold a computer, printer, fax, phone, answering machine, and any other equipment you may need to outfit your home office closet. Choose your equipment wisely. Look into two-in-one—or even three-in-one—pieces of equipment, such as a phone-fax- answering machine combo, or a fax machine that also serves as a printer and scanner. Whatever you chose, a walk-in closet with enough shelves along the walls and storage space below the counters should serve any home office professional well.

Right This artist's office features views from all sides and a wide sliding door to enjoy the sounds and smells of nature. Her spacious studio provides plenty of room to store her supplies, desk, and easel.

The Laundry Room

Sharing space with your washer and dryer may not sound appealing, but when your home office choices are limited, the sounds of the rinse and spin cycle may become soothing. Laundry room set-ups usually include several built-in cabinets surrounding a washer and dryer, and occasionally a small closet. Your technology choices will be limited due to space—unless you have a large laundry room—but a notebook computer, small printer, two-drawer file cabinet, and fax should serve most home office needs. Also, make sure you can run electrical and phone lines in this space.

An Off-the-Patio Office

An off-the-patio home office brings the outdoors in and keeps the elements out. Rather than meet in a stuffy conference room, clients can meet on the patio, take advantage of the gorgeous view, and still conduct business. This type of office is perfect for an artist, architect, or anyone wanting to leave behind the corporate world and get in touch with nature. A simple floor, from concrete to tile to slate, can give an office an informal look while being versatile. One of the best features of an off-the-patio office is the privacy and peace of mind it offers.

BUILT-IN CONSIDERATIONS

If you are planning to stay in your present home for many years, it may be worthwhile to install built-in cabinets, bookshelves, or desks for your office: after all, they are neat, orderly, fairly low-maintenance, and they can really maximize your space. But if you anticipate moving or outgrowing your office at some point in the near (or even not-so-near) future, built-ins are not a good investment. You won't be able to take the furniture with you, and if you're selling your home, it might be more advantageous to feature that spare room as a bedroom than an office. So think carefully before you start measuring for that built-in office!

Under the Stairs

An often-overlooked place for a home office is under the stairs. Using a closet under the stairs as your home office is probably a bad idea due to limited space, poor lighting, and a lack of ventilation. If, however, the space under your stairs is open, all you need is a computer desk or workstation, a two-drawer file cabinet, and plenty of lighting. If the space is near the

entrance to your home, an armoire or other piece of furniture that can be closed when not in use is ideal. You don't want your office to be the first thing people see when they walk into your home, especially if you could stand to organize it better. Keep in mind that if you have toddlers at home, this space may be difficult to use unless your

Below This loft home office turns formerly unused space under the stairs into an efficient storage area. The closed, wooden cabinets offer privacy rarely found in a loft setting.

Opposite top An often-overlooked place for a home office is under the stairs. A corner workstation can house all necessary equipment including a large scanner. Supplies stored in baskets are easy to reach, yet do not interfere with the main workflow.

children spend part of the day with a babysitter.

A Long Hallway

This option involves plenty of creativity. After all, who would consider using their hallway as a home office? When you've outgrown your home and are bursting at the seams, take a close look at your hall. A linen closet along the hallway could be retrofitted with shelves to hold all of your equipment and supplies. This option gives new meaning to closing your office at the end of the day.

A Landing

A landing open to the rest of your home—at least the upstairs—can be an inspiring place to have a home office. Feeling boxed in won't be a problem, although interruptions from family members might be. By adding built-ins and plenty of cabinets, your landing office can be

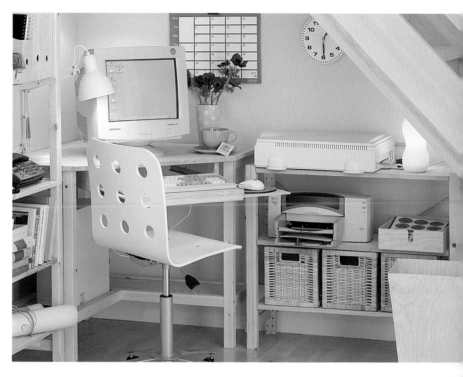

Left Adding a counter to otherwise unused hallway space provides sufficient workspace above and storage below. The rounded-back metal chair fits neatly under the counter when not in use. The movable windows and desk lamp provide enough ambient and task lighting.

Above An open landing with plenty of light and counter space is functional and offers enough room for several staff members. Cabinets placed below the counter and desktop organizers maximize storage space.

Designing Your Office

ONCE YOU'VE DECIDED WHERE TO PUT YOUR HOME OFFICE, you need to think about just how you'll use your space. There's more to think about than just fabrics, color schemes, and styles: this is a room that has to function efficiently and smoothly. Every element—from the floor to the ceiling, the walls to the windows—will have an effect on your working environment. Be sure to consider every option and plan carefully.

Choosing Materials

If you're renovating or creating an entirely new space, there are many choices to be made. In addition to the look and style you like, you need to carefully consider the lighting and sound quality of the room you'll be working in. The typical sounds you find in a corporate office range from coworkers chatting to phones ringing. Within a home office, you may find a similar drone provided by a barking dog, rambunctious children, or a noisy dishwasher. While the corporate sounds are acceptable and at times expected, the home office sounds are not.

If you are building your home office from scratch or remodeling, insulate your walls with fiberglass or other type of insulation that will help to absorb and isolate sound waves. Another option is to add another layer of drywall to decrease the amount of sound that transmits between rooms. Staggering studs between rooms will minimize the amount of sound that passes between rooms.

If you are not interested in tearing up your walls, there are other steps you can take to keep the background noise in your office to a minimum. Start by replacing hollow doors with solid ones that leave a bit of a gap at the bottom for air circulation. Keep in mind also that a bare floor will produce a hollow effect—while talking on the phone, your voice will echo and it may sound like you're in a warehouse. Eliminate the cave effect by adding a few throw rugs or a large area rug to your home office. This will also add color and another design element to your home office.

Replace old, inefficient windows with double-pane or insulated windows. In addition to softening outside noise, you'll improve the look of your home office and conserve energy. Use acoustic ceiling tiles, especially if your home office is in the basement, to minimize noise. A light-colored ceiling tile will brighten your office while cushioning any unwanted background noise.

Consider the light as well. If you have a dull, dreary space, bright, shiny floors can reflect what natural light you have, giving the room a sunnier atmosphere. Also, be careful about choosing colors. A warm shade of cocoa might look wonderful under the fluorescent lights of the home-improvement store, but in your brightly lit office, it might be something else entirely.

Flooring Options

There are so many options available when it comes to choosing flooring for your home office. While wall-to-wall carpeting, area rugs, hardwood flooring, and vinyl tiles are the perennial favorites, other materials ranging from concrete to rubber, and even glass, can also be just what you're looking for when you're laying the groundwork, so to speak, for your home office.

Wall-to-wall carpeting is a simple, fairly low-maintenance choice that provides a soft, warm feeling under foot (a nice touch when you're able to work without shoes). A weekly vacuuming will usually keep it looking great, although light-colored carpets will need to be cleaned more often. And while carpeting your home office will make for better sound-proofing, wall-to-wall carpeting does have its share of disadvantages. For the allergy-prone, carpeting has a tendency to trap irritants, from dust to pollen. It also stains. Of course, if you don't suffer from allergies—or let anyone eat or drink anything in your office—wall-to-wall carpeting could be your best bet.

Hardwood floors are certainly beautiful and in recent years have become much easier to maintain. Track mud into a carpeted home office and then an office with hardwood floors and you'll soon see which one is faster to clean. Hardwood floors, depending on the color of the finish, can lighten the look of a home office and leave you

Below An area rug can soften a room that would otherwise appear harsh and sterile. In addition to minimizing echo on a hard wood floor, a rug adds color and interest to a home office.

with endless choices of window treatments and furniture materials and colors. If your hardwood floor is showing its age with water spots, scuff marks, and the like, refinishing your floor is your best option. Unfortunately, unless you hand-sand your floors, giving them an antiqued or washed look, you will have to deal with a layer of dust in and around your home office. Refinishers may claim to be able to capture all of the dust in their sanding machines, but be skeptical. No matter how efficient the machine, it's still a messy job.

Ceramic tile and stone might sound like practical choices for a floor, but they are probably not the best choice for a home office. Cold and hard, they reflect rather than absorb sound, and are quite expensive to boot. There are alternatives available for those who want the look of stone, marble, or even hardwood, without the maintenance or mess. Today's flooring manufacturers are producing an array of high-quality vinyl and laminate floors that mimic the look of hardwood, stone, marble, or tile, which are easy to install and maintain.

You can have the best of both worlds by laying an area rug over your hardwood, tile, vinyl, or laminate floor. At one time a luxury only afforded by few, area rugs have come down in price and come in more patterns and colors than ever before. Unlike wall-to-wall carpeting, you can move area rugs as you move your furniture. Also, if you want to change your rug, you don't have to pay someone to take out your carpeting and install new carpeting in a different color and material. Cleaning is easier. You can vacuum your rug, and every now and again, take it outside and give it a good beating.

The list of flooring options goes on and on. Materials such as glass and leather are luxurious alternatives, while concrete or rubber flooring can give your home office an industrial effect. Keep an open mind when it comes to flooring in your office. Examine, compare, and contrast everything available to you. You might walk into the flooring store wanting to install wall-to-wall carpeting and come out with an entirely different approach.

FLOORS THAT WORK

Whatever flooring you choose, remember that it's probably going to take a beating. Rolling an office chair from desk to computer workstation and back again will do more damage to hardwood floors than a herd of roller-skating teenagers. Some other surfaces—from stone to shag carpeting—will get in the way of your chair's wheels, and you can't have that, either. That doesn't mean you're limited to vinyl or commercial floors: just invest in a plastic chair mat. Available from office-supply stores and catalogs, these mats are made of translucent hard plastic that sits on your rug or floor and provides a smooth, roller-friendly surface for your work area, while protecting your floors from scratches and gashes, not to mention the occasional coffee spill.

Left **Wall-to-wall
carpeting with
abstract shapes in
various colors brings
dimension and color
to a tiny home office.**

The Walls Around You

Your options for what you'll do with the walls in your office include painting, wallpapering, paneling, tiling—perhaps even carpeting. Your decision depends on the existing condition of your walls, the style you envision for your office, and, perhaps most importantly, the function of the room.

Paint: First of all, consider the walls themselves. Are they drywall or plaster? The quickest and easiest answer is paint. A few days spent on repairing cracks and sanding out bumps and you'll have a beautiful canvas to cover with your favorite color. Or perhaps you're converting a space that was sacrificed to the paneling craze of the late 1960s? A bit of primer and you can turn that faux-wood finish into a bright bit of country beadboard.

Think not only about color but also about finish. Since shiny finishes draw attention to flaws, use a flat or buff finish if your walls are anything less than pristinely smooth. Satin, semigloss, and eggshell finishes offer a smooth and not-too-shiny surface that's still washable. For added texture, consider a special paint treatment for your walls. With the proper tools and a bit of patience, it's easy to create the look of marble, stone, or suede on your walls, or to give them an antique, distressed look.

Wallcovering: Wallpaper is a great way to cover up walls that are not in the best shape and to add texture and visual interest to your space. Try to avoid patterns that are too busy or distracting, and again, think about finish as well as color and design. Before choosing wallpaper, make sure that your walls are smooth; if you have bumps, you'll want to pick a heavier paper with a shiny finish or a design that will camouflage any flaws.

Window Treatments

Whether you have one window in your office space or an entire row of floor-to-ceiling glass, give special consideration to the window treatments you choose. Aside from adding color and texture to your home office, good window treatments provide excellent light control, blocking out harsh light or letting the sunshine in as needed. They also provide privacy, shielding you from the prying eyes of neighbors as you work, and can serve as an effective sound barrier, blocking out outside noise and absorbing any inside noise as well. The type of window treatment you select will depend on where it will be used, how much area you need to cover and, again, your budget. You may choose simple roller shades or plantation shutters. Other shade options include pleated shades, Roman shades, and vertical blinds. Or, you may go for a more traditional, romantic approach and hang curtains or drapes in your home office space. The choice is yours.

Shades versus Blinds: Shades are available in a variety of styles, from fancy Roman shades to simple paper or bamboo shades that are available for just a few dollars. While they are great for privacy, they are not the best choice for light control, as they do not offer any kind of light filtration. Blinds, on the other hand, provide excellent light control and privacy. Both horizontal, or venetian, blinds and vertical blinds allow you to control the amount of light you want to let into the room and at least partially reduce outside noise. They can be on the expensive side, however, so you may want to look into some of your other options before committing to vertical blinds. They range in price from quite expensive for custom-made treatments to downright cheap for ready-made examples for standard sized windows.

WALLS THAT WORK FOR YOU

Once you've decided how to treat your walls, it's time to think about how you'll use them. Are you a graphic artist who will need lots of space to review compositions? Consider covering one or more walls entirely in cork—it will give you a versatile gallery space to review your ideas, and you'll be able to add and remove them without marring your walls. Or, if you're short on space, use wall-mounted storage units to stow disks, books, and other tools of your trade. Don't forget about decorative touches; you'll be spending a lot of time within those walls, so be sure to hang a pretty picture or decorative mirror to make your space a bit more comfortable and pleasing.

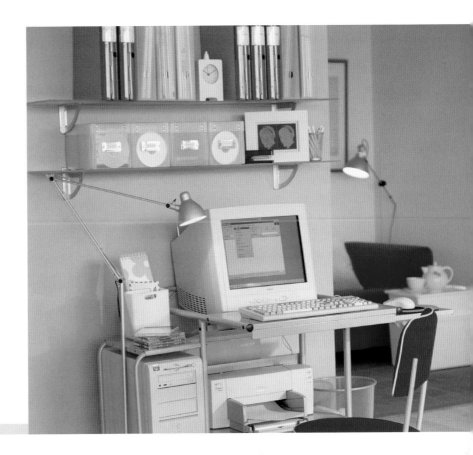

A pleated shade is the most versatile type of window treatment because it can be raised from the bottom or lowered from the top, depending on where you want the light to come in. It's not the best option when it comes to sound block-ing, but it is a less-expensive altern-ative then some of the other window treatment options available.

Other Treatments: Plantation shutters are ideal for controlling the amount of light you bring into your home office. In addition to giving your home office a light, airy atmosphere, they make great sound barriers. They may also change the look of an otherwise plain office, depending on the color and type of material you select. Adding a balloon shade will dress up the shutters and tie in the other fabrics and colors within your home office.

While thick drapes are somewhat rare these days, they are one of the most effective sound barriers available. The downside is that if you want to work in a quiet office, you'll have to keep them closed and do without natural light. Breezy linen curtains won't do much in the way of sound blockage, but they will give your space a romantic feel and filter harsh sunlight. If your office is located over a quiet courtyard and blocking out noise is not an issue, these might be an ideal solution. Whatever you decide, be sure that your window treatments complement the décor of your home office in style, fabric, and material.

Design Plan Checklist

- Measure each wall (including alcoves).

- Include all windows, doorways, vents, and closets.

- Don't forget any immovable objects including columns (mostly found in basements).

- Do a rough sketch of your office and plug in all measurements.

- Redraw the sketch to scale. You may also transfer the sketch to a computer program, or give the sketch to a space planner or architect if you want to make structural improvements and aren't comfortable doing them yourself.

- Measure your furniture and arrange it on the graph paper or on your computer program.

- Determine whether you need more storage space and if so, add an armoire or storage cabinet to your plan.

Designing Your Workspace

Your home office plan can be as simple or elaborate as you like, depending on whether you're going to upgrade your furniture and equipment, remodel an existing office, or create an entirely new home office from the ground up. A furniture or equipment upgrade is a project you can handle alone, but when you start looking into built-ins or new construction, consider bringing others into the fold. A contractor, space planner, or architect can give you good ideas regarding the potential for your chosen home office space.

Whether you plan your office using graph paper and a pencil or invest in a computer layout program, you can't plan your office until you have a clear picture in your mind of how you want it to look. Start by measuring each wall, window opening, doorway, closet, and alcove in your home office. Measure the room at least twice to make sure you haven't missed or mismeasured anything.

Do a rough sketch in pencil that includes vents and any other openings that shouldn't be blocked with furniture. Any permanent item, such as a column or circuit breaker panel, needs to be included and not blocked. Redraw the sketch to scale using graph paper (the bigger the better) and pencil or transfer your drawing to your computer program. You may be more comfortable handing this part of the project over to a space planner or architect. If you will be making structural changes, put as much detail into your drawing as possible. In most cases, a professional will come to your home office and measure it again, but by doing the drawing, you can decide if you want to hire an architect or space planner or take on the project yourself.

Left If you have lots of papers and projects you need to spread out, a simple computer workstation may not be enough. Here, the connecting corner of the L-shape arrangement provides additional room for storing a desk lamp out of the way, while keeping it close enough to provide vital task lighting. The small, yet useful, hutch keeps the computer-desk portion of the "L" partially free and serves as a handy storage place for frequently accessed supplies.

The next step is to measure your furniture (or the furniture that you are considering purchasing) and create to-scale paper models that you can push around the graph paper to see if everything fits. Or, photocopy your drawing and make a few versions showing your furniture arranged differently in each drawing. You may find that your furniture is too large for your new office—or even too small if you're setting up in a large space. Whatever the case, by taking the time to arrange your furniture, you will have a clear picture of how your office will look and what you will need to furnish it.

OLD OFFICE, NEW OFFICE

Think back to the many workspaces you've had during the course of your career and decide which one worked best for you. Within your first cubicle, was everything within arm's reach? Or perhaps you found that being able to lean back in your office chair and put your feet up really got your creative juices flowing? Did you work better with your desk facing the doorway, window, or wall? Remember to consider what tasks you handled in the space: that little cubicle might have been great when you were a young sales assistant whose tasks were limited to typing correspondence and making phone calls, but as a work-at-home sales rep, you might find that you need more space to spread out.

The Right Arrangement

Even the most elegant furniture, with inlaid patterns and sleek curves, is only as functional as its setup. Placing a desk against one wall, a file cabinet out of arm's reach, and a bookcase on the other end of your office unfortunately creates a mini workout room involving constant movement to and from various parts of your office. By creating a compact, yet not-too-confined work area, everything you need will be within reach and you won't waste time jumping from area to area.

There are six basic arrangements for your home office. The arrangement you choose will depend on the size of your office, the type of furniture you have, and how much work surface you need. Keep in mind that if someone else is sharing your office, your choices may be limited.

L-Shape

The L-shaped work area offers the important advantage of moving your equipment off your desk and onto a secondary surface. For example, on a computer stand perpendicular to your desk (or credenza that you could use as a writing surface), you could place your monitor, keyboard, printer, and fax and place your CPU

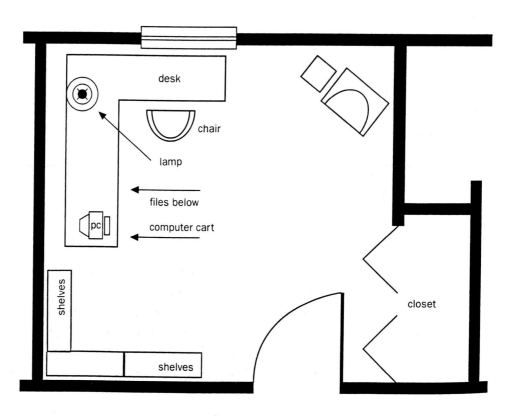

Above **L-shaped work area.**

underneath. The advantage of a credenza over a standard desk is more file drawers. The only disadvantage to the L-shape is lack of an additional open space to work. If you have the room, you may consider adding an extra surface to create a U-shape (see right). However, if you know you'll probably only use the extra surface to store unnecessary items and clutter up your work area, stick with the L-shape.

Furniture options for creating an L-shape include a two-piece unit with a desk and return attached. You could create your own L-shape with a computer desk and credenza or computer desk and worktable or desk with a computer workstation. There are several ways you can configure an L-shape. Your only limitations are your furniture choices.

If you use two pieces of furniture to create the L, add a floor lamp in between the pieces in the corner, a tall live or artificial tree, or a printer stand. Your furniture pieces don't have to be edge to edge to qualify as an L.

U-Shape

This arrangement allows you to keep everything within reach on three surfaces. You might put a computer workstation that houses all of your electronic equipment to the left of your desk. To the right you might have a credenza, table, or lateral file cabinet with a fax machine, and a telephone-answering machine combination. A stand-alone phone could be placed on your desk in front of you if you don't want to use your fax phone, or if you have a separate line for business, which is recommended. This layout is extremely convenient. All you have to do is swivel your chair one way or the other while you work. The only disadvantage to this arrangement is that it requires more space than an L-shaped arrangement.

Create the U-shape by using any of the configurations just described, or add another work surface including a credenza, standard desk, or computer cart. Avoid mixing and matching too

many different styles of furniture. A melamine desk with an oak credenza, mixed with a chrome or steel computer cart will give your office a "thrown-together" look. This look may not bother you, especially if you know clients will not be visiting your office. You might just choose random pieces of furniture from throughout your home to use in your office. If you're starting from scratch, match the furniture as much as you can, especially if you will be meeting with clients in your office. The style of furniture doesn't necessarily have to match, just the color scheme and materials.

Above **A U-shape configuration provides a main work surface and two additional surfaces for spreading out papers and storing frequently used resources and equipment. The top left- or right-hand section of the U is a good place for a computer, making use of an otherwise dead space.**

Below Built-in file cabinets and a desk on wheels are ideal for creating a workable, parallel arrangement. The light desk chair can be moved to the other side of the desk when a project requires constant referral to the files stored behind, or for a change of pace.

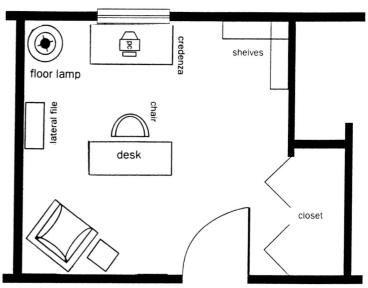

Above **Parallel work area.**

Above A counter arrangement doesn't have to be perfectly square. In fact, it's more interesting with a little shape—and texture. This author's crescent-shape brick desk includes the bare essentials and plenty of workspace.

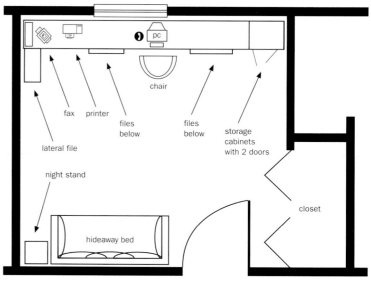

Above **Counter arrangement.**

The Parallel Work Area

With this layout, your desk or primary work surface faces into the room and your secondary surface is behind you. Although the two surfaces aren't next to each other, you can easily access everything you need. One surface could be your computer desk that also holds your fax, while the other is for your phone, files, and supplies you use daily or weekly. Another option is to have a traditional desk that holds the items you use often and a credenza as a secondary surface. The parallel layout has some of the same disadvantages as the L-shape, including fewer surfaces to work on.

The Counter Arrangement

If you install counters along one wall, or combine built-ins with a long table, the effect is one long work surface. Not only will you have space to work on the counter but plenty of storage space below when you add a few two-drawer file cabinets and cabinets with shelves. An articulating keyboard will put your keyboard at the right height and your keyboard will store out of the way when not in use. A light, laminate surface will give your office a clean look, although there are many styles of laminate countertops available. The main disadvantage of a light countertop is glare. If your counter is directly across from the window, the surface may reflect too much light. To avoid that problem use a black counter or dark surface. You also could add a desk blotter to block out glare.

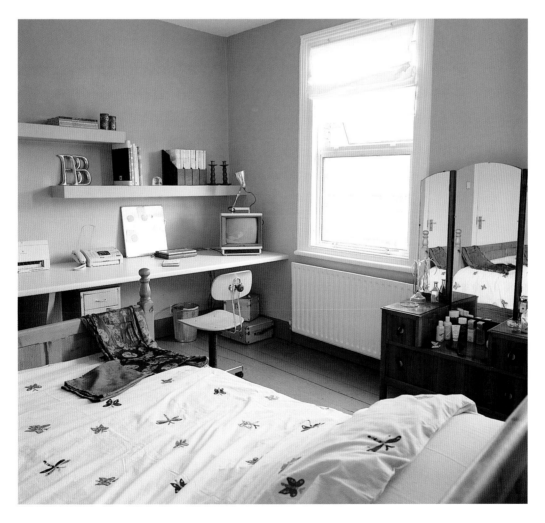

Left **The staggered shelves above this counter arrangement keep reference materials within reach and provide a place for displaying personal items. The large window at a right angle to this robin's-egg-blue counter setup brings in natural light for the work area, but not too much light for the sleeping area. The rolling supply cart stored below the desk occupies little space while holding additional supplies and files.**

Top A corner arrangement.

Bottom A large corner arrangement includes extra workspace on either side of the computer. The CPU stored on the floor in the corner is out of the way, yet still accessible. A large mirror near the printer opens up the space, while a large transom window brings in natural light.

The Corner Arrangement

When you were in school, being stuck in a corner was a bad thing. But in your home office, the corner can be the most inspirational area of the room. With the right furniture—a unit designed to fit in your corner—you can have room to store your computer equipment and still have space to work. This arrangement doesn't work in every office, especially if you don't have a corner long enough on each side to place your furniture. Or, you may have a room in which one wall is long enough, but the other wall is covered with low windows or a door to the outside. A corner arrangement would not work in this space.

The Reverse Corner Arrangement

The V-shaped arrangement lets you face out with your desk on one side of you and your return on the other. Instead of facing the corner of your home office, your desk and return faces toward the room, meaning all sides of the furniture needs to be finished (unfinished particle board on the back side of your furniture can't be camouflaged unless you want to attach cork board and turn the part facing your office into a large bulletin board). If you hold frequent meetings, this arrangement is perfect. You can add desk chairs to the sides of your arrangement. Some units have a rounded desk on the end for conducting meetings.

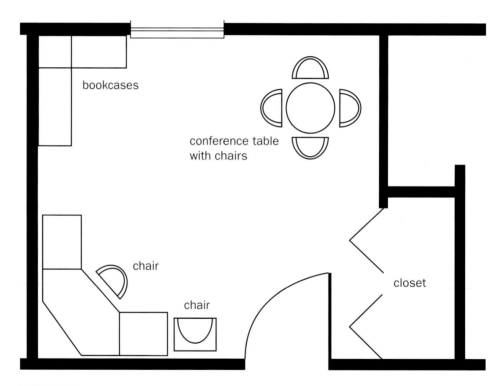

Left **A reverse corner arrangement on the second floor gives the office a treehouse effect with windows that parallel outside transom windows. An abundance of counter space, shelves, and cabinets ensures that everything is within reach.**

Below **A reverse corner arrangement.**

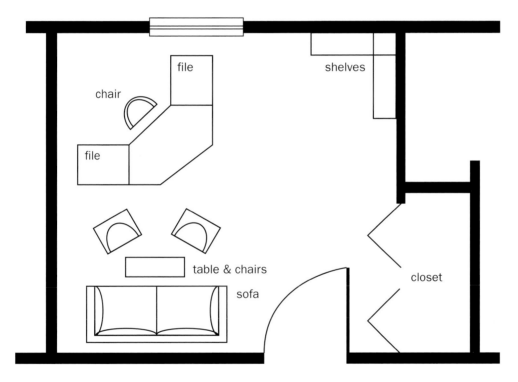

file

chair

file

shelves

closet

table & chairs

sofa

Getting Down to Business
Putting Your Home Office to Work

When it comes to home offices, designing the perfect space is only the beginning. You need to choose furnishings that will be comfortable enough to work in for hours at a time and create systems that will keep you organized and efficient. Perhaps most importantly, you need to develop your work habits and adjust to working at home. Your work, your attitude, and the appearance of your office must send a clear message to colleagues and clients that although you work at home, you are a true professional and your work is a business, not a hobby.

This section addresses the business of the business, from choosing and paying for furnishings and equipment to creating systems for staying organized to

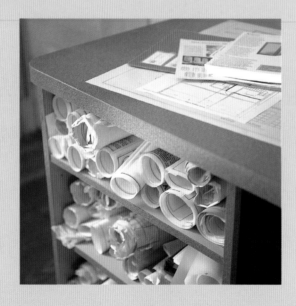

stocking and storing office supplies. You'll also find guidance for the specific challenges of working at home, such as working and playing in dual-function rooms, keeping home and work clearly separated, and entertaining clients in your home.

It's important to remember that the way you design your office will affect the way you run your business, and vice versa. Your space should reflect not only the way that you work but the work that you do and the professionalism with which you do it.

Setting up Shop

PULLING TOGETHER ALL THE ELEMENTS OF YOUR HOME OFFICE, from floor to ceiling, desk to file cabinets, and from computer to pencils, can be a heady task. You need to determine what you need, what you want, and what you can really have. After all, a business won't last long if you spend more than you earn. Think about the different ways you can design your space, consider the materials and furnishings you already may have, and prioritize every purchase, from furniture and equipment down to pencils and erasers. Treat every purchase like a business decision.

Sticking to Your Budget

Of course, the bottom line is the most important aspect of any business, at home or out in the corporate world. Of course, you have to spend a bit of money before you can earn any, but a home-based business will not last long if you spend indiscriminately on renovations, furniture, equipment, and décor. That's why it's imperative that you set up a strict budget at the onset, and stick to it. Figure out how much you need to spend to get your business started, estimate how much money you'll be earning out of your office, and set your budget accordingly. It's possible to keep your initial cash outlay to a minimum and build your office slowly as you start earning money.

First Things First: Prioritize

Start with the bare essentials: computer, worktable, and phone line. Head to your local copy shop to print, fax, and copy; use the library rather than investing in reference books. Then allocate a specific monthly budget for office supplies, furniture, and equipment and add to your office over time. As your business picks up and more income begins rolling in, you can adjust the amount you're spending on the office accordingly.

Of course, some businesses will require a more significant cash outlay up front. A freelance writer, for example, might get by for a while with a secondhand laptop computer setup on the dining room table, but a graphic designer might have to invest in a faster, more up-to-date machine as well as programs costing almost a thousand dollars each. So it's important to figure out what your needs are and prioritize each purchase. Identify what you need to start up, what you'll need once your business is rolling, and what you'd like to get once you've started turning a profit.

This kind of plan has many advantages. First, you won't have to lay out as much cash at the beginning, when your business is just getting started and money will be tight, especially if you've just given up a steady paycheck. Second, by working without certain items for a while, you will get a better sense of what you really need. For example, you might find that you rely on e-mail heavily but rarely need to go to the copy shop to fax—so invest in a faster Internet connection and forgo the fax machine altogether. You might also find that your weekly or daily trip to the copy shop provides a nice break and a cure for cabin fever.

Finally, by working in your bare-bones office, you'll get a sense of what kind of configuration works for you before you invest in any furniture. So you won't realize that an L-shaped workstation is what really works for you only after you've put a significant amount of money into a fancy, all-in-one computer armoire.

Waste Not, Want Not

Even if your office-supply budget is unlimited, you'll waste money and storage space buying items that you don't need and probably don't have room to store anyway. Before you buy anything for your office, make sure that the item will serve a specific purpose, and more importantly, that you don't already own the item. Start by knowing what you have, where it's stored, and if you have room to store additional supplies and equipment. Otherwise, the item may end up in your garage long before your monthly credit card statement arrives.

Shop around for the best prices on anything and everything you buy for your home office. Buy items you use often (paper, tape, and mailing supplies) in bulk, and be sure to check out warehouse clubs as well as office-supply superstores. You can save time and money by

Opposite This anything-but-traditional home office features top-of-the-line storage using rich and functional materials. The marble-top rolling file cart provides ample file space, while the baskets fastened to the near-by steel pole offer additional open storage space. Three tall wooden cabinets, filled with supplies and reference materials, make it easier to keep any clutter under control and behind doors.

shopping on-line: look for stores that provide free shipping for large orders, and make your purchases all at once. Investigate sales and rebates. Whether you are buying supplies on-line or in person, buy supplies in advance as much as possible so you never have to waste valuable time running to the nearest 24-hour drugstore or convenience store to buy a new printer cartridge to finish a project.

Finally, save all your receipts. Not only will you need them come tax time, but they are a valuable tool for tracking expenses, helping you figure out just how much paper you're using, or how long a printer cartridge lasts for you, all of which help you to set realistic budget parameters. Plus, if you keep the receipt, you'll be able to return any equipment that you find you don't need or doesn't work for you.

Furnishing Your Home Office

Choosing your furnishings—specifically, your desk and storage units—must be done with care. Consider not only what you've determined to be your optimal setup but the style, quality, and flexibility of each unit you look at. Office fur-niture has come a long way from the flimsy, cheap computer desks and workstations that home office professionals of the past had no other choice but to use. Cheap workstations still exist, but they're easy to spot with their unbelievably low prices and shoddy construction to match. Fortunately, as the needs and businesses of home office professionals have changed, so has the furniture available to them. Today's home office professional has a choice of many high-quality, well-designed, and functional furniture options—from custom-made to ready-

made to homemade—that will not only blend in with, but complement, their décor.

As you consider your options, keep in mind that your home office doesn't have to reflect the corporate office you just left (or feared being trapped inside for at least eight hours a day). Instead, your home office can be a reflection of you and your interests, tastes, and design sense. A large part of this will be reflected in the kinds of furniture you select. Before you buy anything, check for quality. You may be getting a bargain at the time, but if you have to replace the same item several times because it keeps falling apart, it's not much of a bargain. Remember: You generally get what you pay for.

Solid-Wood Furniture

The most expensive of all types of furniture is solid wood. Its look is unmatched by any other type of material, but if cost is a consideration, solid wood may out of the question. If your budget is unlimited or higher than the average home-office professional, you can buy furniture in oak, maple, walnut, and pine—the latter being easy to scratch. Keep in mind that you can spend thousands of dollars on furniture that looks impressive, but if it lacks enough storage and workspace for your purposes, it is not going to be effective in your home office. By all means, look for quality wood furniture—but don't forget about function.

Wood Veneer

How can you still get a solid wood look, without spending a fortune? Many manufacturers produce pieces using wood veneer (wood adhered to particleboard) instead of solid wood. Higher-end pieces use $3\frac{1}{3}$ inches (1.3 cm) thick particleboard, while less expensive models use $1\frac{1}{8}$ inches (2.9 cm). Also, the veneer on the higher-end pieces is thicker than the thin, shelf-paper-like vinyl covering found on low-end

OFFICE IN A BOX

Rather than use your home address for your business address, rent a postal suite (for example The UPS Store) or use a P.O. box. Postal regulations have changed, making it necessary to use a number sign (#) or PMB (postal mailbox) instead of a suite number, but using another address has a few advantages:

- Clients and especially sales people won't make unexpected visits to your home office.
- The postal staff can accept packages for you, which is a major convenience when you are out of town (or out to lunch, at the gym, or just taking a day off).
- Using a postal address looks professional and gives the impression that your business is bigger than it really is (even though you have to add the number sign or PMB instead of suite after the address).
- You won't have to worry about your family mixing your business mail with your personal correspondence.

pieces. Higher-end pieces use HCL (high-compression laminate), while the lower end uses LCL (low-compression laminate). When con-sidering furniture with wood veneers, test how sturdy the piece is and how it is constructed. If it's an RTA (ready-to-assemble) piece, you'll know exactly how it is put together. If not, check the drawers for smooth drawer glides and see if the pieces have been solidly attached.

Glass and Steel

If you're looking for more contemporary (and affordable) furniture, take a close look at a combination glass-steel setup. Whether you want a black or gray steel base, you can get a more formal (with black) or a casual (with gray) look. The downside with glass is glare and fingerprints. One solution is to invest in a desk blotter. And if the fingerprints really bug you, keep a bottle of glass cleaner and a rag nearby (and out of the reach of small children).

Right **A compact, efficient, and simple computer workstation makes a small space go a long way. Shelves above this all-alminum workstation on wheels make any open area fair game for a home office.**

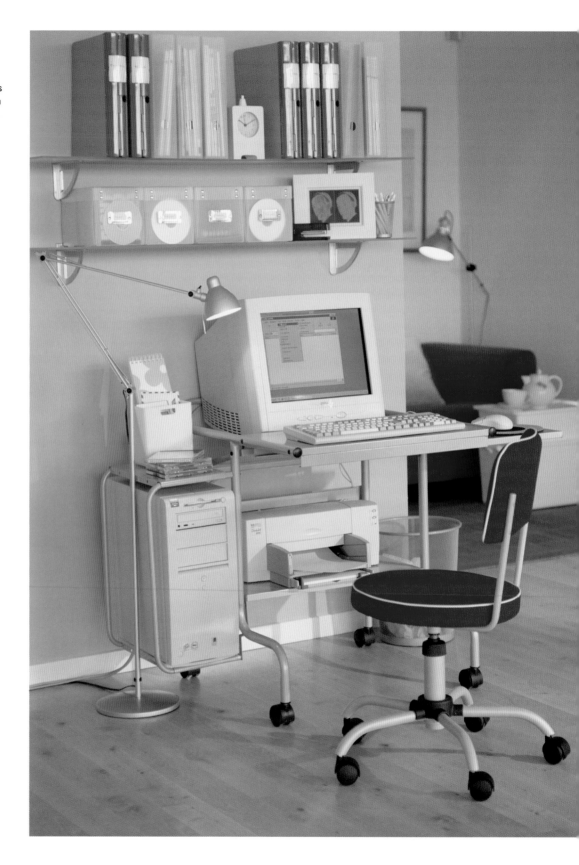

Functional Furniture with an Ergonomic Edge

Many corporations find that ergonomically designed workstations, chairs, and other equipment are worthwhile investments: workers who are comfortable are more productive. What's more, workers who spend hours tooling away in front of a computer at poorly designed workstations or in improper chairs risk serious health problems, including such repetitive stress injuries as Carpal Tunnel Syndrome, and myriad back problems, the costs of which—in terms of liability and productivity—far outweigh the price of well-designed equipment.

The same considerations should be taken into account when designing your home office. You'll be more inclined to work at a comfortable desk, in a chair that provides proper support, and you'll get more done with equipment that doesn't stress your body. Even more important, work-related injuries stemming from poorly designed furniture and even accessories can affect not just your productivity, but your long-term health, no matter where you work. The risk is even greater for those who work at home—after all, there's no corporation to hold liable for your injuries and there are no sick days for the self-employed. That's why choosing your furniture and equipment carefully is imperative.

Finding the Perfect Workstation

All-in-one setups in any of the configurations outlined in Carving Out a Space are available in a range of styles and prices; you can save a great deal of money by purchasing units that you put together yourself. Shop carefully when investigating prefabricated workstations, and think about your specific needs. Look for features like built-in electrical outlets and cord tamers, rollout

Ergonomic Tip Sheet

- Place equipment in positions that place minimal strain on your neck, shoulders, arms, and back.

- Use proper lighting and eliminate glare.

- Chose halogen lights for task lighting.

- Invest in ergonomic keyboards, wrist supports, copy trays, and lumbar cushions; investigate alternatives to the standard computer mouse.

- Buy the best chair you can afford.

- Your work surface should be 28 inches (71 cm) high, and the keyboard height should be adjustable, between 23 inches (58 cm) and 27 inches (68 cm).

- Inclined surfaces are better for writing, drawing, or marking anything by hand.

- A hands-free headset for your phone allows you to talk while typing or taking notes without hunching up your shoulders or straining your neck.

- An adjustable footrest takes pressure off of your knees and ankles while you work.

Top This functional table spends part of the day as a desk and the other as a conference table.

Middle A rolling file/storage cart keeps files and supplies within reach. Whether stored next to or under a desk, frequently used files are only inches away within a portable cart.

Bottom This office may be small, yet it provides plenty of wall and surface storage. As computer equipment continues to shrink, the ability to work in a small space grows.

keyboard trays, and dust-free compartments for your CPU, printer, or scanner. Bring along the precise measurements of your space to make sure that the unit will fit well. Most importantly, bring along a list of the equipment you'll need to accommodate and make sure that there's a place for everything. Is there a space for a tower CPU, rather than the desktop model you've got? Is there a place to store files?

If you can't seem to find the unit that precisely suits your needs, or you simply don't want to spend a lot of money, there are plenty of options available. With a bit of creativity, you could build your own desk and workstation using modular units or even errant pieces of furniture. Do you have an old antique secretary gathering dust? With no room for a computer or to spread out papers, it might be outdated as a primary workspace, but with its clever cubbies and ample drawer space, it's far from obsolete. Consider putting it to work as a spot to sort mail and write out bills and phone messages; use the drawers to store office supplies like tape, staples, pens, and pencils. If you need a place to

spread out, take a trip to your local home-improvement store and pick up a pair of sawhorses and a plywood door to create a simple trestle-style desk. Install a rollout keyboard attachment (available at office-supply stores) beneath the desktop, and add a coat of paint in your choice of color and finish, and you've got a sleek, modern, and totally functional workspace.

Whether you're buying a ready-made workstation, having a built-in one installed, or building one yourself, you'll want your workstation to be ergonomically correct. Many of the newer

premade units already are (see Ergonomic Tip Sheet). An articulating keyboard that adjusts for height and angle is essential. Some keyboards come with a slide-out mouse tray as well. If you still do a lot of writing by hand, for instance grading papers or editing manuscripts, consider installing an inclined work surface, which eases pressure on your neck and reduces strain on your eyes. By all means, give all your office furniture a test-drive before you buy: sit at the station and swivel around in the chair. Can you reach everything? Is there enough room to sit back? To stretch your legs?

The All-Important Chair

An office chair is one of the most important things you'll buy for your home office, yet it is often the most overlooked. The more time you spend in front of your computer, the more you need to focus on finding the right chair that fits your frame, is mobile (for reaching files and supplies), and fits the décor of your office. The more features you need in a chair, the more money you're going to spend, but keep in mind that your chair is an investment. A higher-quality chair is worth the money you spend, as chairs take a beating and cheap ones just don't hold up for long. What's more, extra money spent on your chair is money saved on doctor visits to treat recurring back pain and muscle strain caused by an inferior chair.

The type of chair you buy is limited only by your budget (often the deciding factor), design taste, and needs. Design-wise, there are many choices, from retro chairs to traditional, high-back chairs. While chairs with high backs, wooden arm rests, and smooth wood finishes give a home office a sleek, polished look, ergonomic-wise, they tend to fail the function, comfort, and longevity test. Fortunately, you can find an office chair that is both appealing and functional. Look for these qualities: 1) Lumbar support to reduce the strain on your lower back; 2) a waterfall seat, meaning that the front edge of the seat is rounded to prevent restricted circulation and compression of nerves behind your knees; 3) adjustable seat and back height; 4) tilt mechanisms and tilt lock to reduce strain and fatigue of your leg muscles; and 5) tension control that adjusts to your body weight for easier reclining.

Any type of office chair is better than using a kitchen or dining room chair. And office and medical supply stores offer a variety of cushions that can improve the ergonomic function of an existing chair. Regardless of how much you have to spend, it pays to buy the best office chair that you can afford. Try any chair before you buy it to see if it fits your frame, matches your color scheme, and is in proportion with the rest of your office; if you are buying furniture online, look for a retailer that has the item in stock, and try it out first. Better yet, look for a supplier with a money-back guarantee, because you really don't know if a chair will work for you until you've had a chance to sit in it for a good, long stretch.

Below A nontraditional office chair combines style and function in an ergonomically correct, comfortable chair. A chair should conform to the user with adjustable supports, such as armrests, a backrest, tilt and swivel options.

LIGHTING doesn't have to be an either-or proposition. Instead of using one type of light, layer the lighting. You can use indirect lighting fixtures to create an ambient layer and fluorescent light strips to light spaces that have no ceiling or wall access for electric service. Then add task lighting wherever it's needed. Fluorescents are a good choice, but halogen lights, which provide bright task lighting without glare, are even better. Use these definitions to familiarize yourself with the three types of lighting you can use for your home office: general or background illumination, focal or task lighting, and accent or decorative lighting.

Layered Lighting

GENERAL ILLUMINATION is also called background or ambient lighting; it is usually the foundation of a lighting plan. It should be used to compensate for lack of natural light during the day, and it should provide uniform illumination throughout a room at night. This uniform illumination is usually provided by ceiling fixtures, but can also be created with a variety of light sources placed around a room that form overlapping pools of light, such as floor and table lamps; up- and downlights; or sidelights, sconces, and spots. While it can be dull and flat or harsh and glaring, overall general illumination should be shadowless, not accentuating anything particular about a space. Instead, it should project a sense of homogeneity in an office and be reassuring and restful.

FOCAL OR TASK LIGHTING is directive—it creates a bright spot that draws our attention, tells us what to look at, or orients us toward an important element or activity center in a space. It is bright, concentrated, and directed to allow office activities to be accomplished with safety and ease. However, task lighting also creates shadows around the objects in its field because of the intensity of illumination it throws off. Make sure that the shadows don't fall over the work area; situate the light source in front of or to the side of a person rather than behind him. Lamps with long, flexible heads, necks, or arms create this type of lighting. If shades that are open at the top and bottom (as opposed to highly targeted and closed) are used, focal lighting can also supplement the general illumination in a room.

ACCENT OR DECORATIVE LIGHTING is any bright light directed into or onto a specific area for aesthetic rather than utilitarian effect. Use accent lighting in a client-friendly office space, to enhance or emphasize significant features or furnishings such as architectural elements, shelves, armoires, collections of objects, and art. Accent lighting can have an unwavering focus to highlight with glamour and drama, or it can wash over a broader area, such as an entire wall or architectural element, for an emphasis that is obvious but more subtle. In general, accent lighting should be at least three times brighter than the room's general lighting. Any fixture that can be trained to shine light in one specific direction can be used for this type of lighting. However, if it is too bright, the purpose of bringing nuance and contrast to a space is defeated. For this reason, it is advisable to out-fit accent lights with dimmers so they can be adjusted if necessary.

Above A well-lit office reduces fatigue and eyestrain. Between the natural light filtering in from the floor-to-ceiling windows, and with overhead lighting above the seating area, spot lighting over the bookcases, and task lighting on the desk, all areas of this office can be illuminated.

Working in a Whole New Light

Are you fatigued or overworked? Eyestrain and low productivity can be blamed on many things, but the main culprit may be a lack of good lighting. While some people prefer to work with minimal light, letting the monitor serve as the primary light source, others want every area of their workspace bright. Fortunately, there is more than one way to light your home office: ambient or general lighting; natural lighting; fluorescent (which is non-flickering, unlike the kind found in old office buildings); task lighting; and accent lighting (used more for atmosphere than working). You can use one or a combination of these lighting sources to achieve the

right amount of light. For more information on each of these types of lighting, refer to Layered Lighting on page 73.

Determine the tasks that need to be lit before you select the proper lighting. Start by identifying the most important areas and consider what tasks you will perform and where you will perform each task. Do you frequently read marketing reports at your desk? Is filing important? Are you in front of the computer most of the day? Task lighting will help you see paper and your keyboard and can be accomplished by using halogen or fluorescent adjustable-arm desk lights or under-cabinet lighting. A standard, clip-on lamp or gooseneck lamp will provide a source

Top left A toy-like, bendable lamp is functional and fun. Fortunately, a lamp doesn't have to be large to light wide areas effectively.

Top right This steel lamp with a plated satin finish brings a retro feel to a home office, while bathing the desk in light.

Center An adjustable lamp, able to move easily where it's needed, can be folded and pushed out of the way when not in use. A heavy, weighted base keeps the lamp stable and eliminates any unexpected toppling.

Bottom right A translucent lamp available in multiple shades brings color and an interesting contrast to traditional desk lighting. The shade arm adjusts to reach 32 inches (81 cm) high and the 11 inches (28 cm) long shade swivels to shine light across the keyboard or desk area.

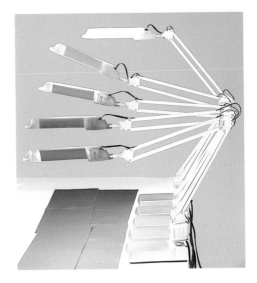

of task lighting that won't be in your way. If you are right-handed, keep the task light on your left side; if left-handed, do the opposite. Installing lighting underneath built-in wall cabinets will provide an unobtrusive but effective light source.

If you need more light than what your windows can provide (which you will), or have to shut your blinds in the morning if your windows and monitor face the sunrise, you still will have access to ambient light with an overhead fixture or track lighting. Too much overhead light, for example from a fixture attached to a ceiling fan, can cause glare on your screen, so adjust the lighting accordingly. A halogen floor lamp provides overall lighting and is ideal set in a corner of your office. Equipped with a dimmer switch, it provides an adjustable source of lighting that can illuminate the entire room.

The Ergonomically Friendly Computer

The Information Age has taken workers out of the coal mines and off of the assembly lines, and plopped them down in front of computer keyboards. While our new surroundings may seem a great deal safer than the conditions our grandparents endured, those of us who spend countless hours working on computers are actually at risk for some serious health problems. In addition to finding the proper chair, workstation, and lighting, there are some simple adjustments that you should keep in mind when setting up and sitting at your computer.

The placement of your computer is one of the first things to consider. Your monitor should be at a right angle to a window to avoid glare. If you have to place your monitor with a window behind you, use some type of window treatment to cut down on glare; a glare screen will cut down on glare from your monitor too. If the monitor will be in front of a window, the same advice applies, to avoid having to adjust your eyes between the light coming from the window and the monitor. Keep your monitor at a comfortable height, directly in front of the keyboard: you should not have to turn your neck while you're working in order to see what you're doing. The correct viewing angle is 10 degrees to 30 degrees below eye level. If you need to refer to books or copy while you work, invest in a copyholder or bookstand that will hold your papers upright so that you won't have to strain to read them. If your budget isn't too stretched, invest in a thin, flat-screen monitor that takes up less room than a standard monitor, cuts glare to a large degree, and swivels (it also

frees up desk space for other uses).

Experiment with different styles of keyboards. While the standard keyboard that comes with most computers might seem perfectly fine, a split-key design will ease the pressure on your wrists and elbows by gently moving your arms away from your torso. Add a cushioned wrist rest for added support. Likewise, think about replacing your mouse with a rollerball or touchpad; requiring only minimal movement of the thumbs, these tools eliminate the sore shoulders and arms caused by manipulating a mouse all day.

Opposite The brushed metal, two-in-one torchiere (left) provides general lighting for this office and task lighting for the reading area. The overhead lamp piggybacks with the desk lamp to provide additional desktop lighting.

Below What this office lacks in warmth, it makes up in ergonomics. From the adjustable monitor stand and desktop, to the wrist rest and mouse rest, this office helps reduce wrist, neck, and back injuries.

Storage Solutions

When it comes to storage space, few home offices can claim to have too much. Before you resign yourself to storing extra supplies, samples, and reference materials in other parts of your home, think creatively. Do you have a piece of furniture that both complements the décor of your office and could do double duty as office-supply storage? If you added shelves to a spare bedroom closet, you could store books, supplies, and even a file cabinet inside (depending on the depth of the closet and the height of the cabinet), leaving room outside for additional furniture and equipment. Not having enough space is one problem, but not using the existing space to its maximum potential is another. It's not uncommon to see wasted space in a home office that could be better utilized and designed.

Left Plastic containers filled with supplies make efficient use of the space below the stairs. Even the copier, normally an item that takes up valuable counter space, has a convenient home in one of the drawers.

Basic Home Office Equipment

EQUIPPING your office with the tools necessary for your business doesn't have to blow your budget. Start with these basics and as your business grows or needs change, add to or upgrade these items.

- Computer system with monitor, keyboard, and modem.

- Ink-jet or laser printer.

- Stand-alone fax (if not within your computer) or multi-function peripheral (fax, copier, and printer).

- Backup system (CD/RW, Zip, Jazz, or tape drive).

- Desktop lamp for task lighting.

- Smoke detector and fire extinguisher.

- Telephone with voice mail or answering system.

Right A loft office with open shelves is ideal for the "look-out" who fears "out of sight, out of mind." Similar supplies are stored together on shelves, while files are in one central area below. The CPU suspended under the desk and a file holder on the floor keeps the desk relatively clear. The multicolored window panes and the yellow chairs create warmth in the steel, aluminum, and wood decor.

Opposite **Magazines neatly stored in labeled magazine holders keep publications within reach, while adding an interesting design element to this office. The magazines are cataloged by publication and year and replaced each month with the corresponding issue for the current month.**

Left **An angled bookcase keeps supplies organized in boxes of varying sizes and materials and within reach. Heavier items are stored on the bottom shelf to balance the weight.**

STOW IT, TOTE IT, ROLL IT AWAY

Some of the best storage solutions are also among the least expensive and most adaptable and can be found at your local hardware or housewares store. Multicolored milk crates are ideal for holding magazines, books, videotapes, and CDs—stack them to create a bookcase effect or place them in various parts of your office, on their sides, to make it easy to see what is inside. Sturdy, molded-plastic rolling carts with clear drawers eliminate clutter and make finding what you need simple. Rubber-coated, metal rolling carts have the added feature of being able to switch the size of the basket or drawer you currently have. If you need more file space, you can add a deeper basket. Ready-made closet-customization kits can divvy up your closet space to meet your specific needs.

ADD TO THIS LIST any supplies that are specific to your business and delete those that do not apply. Then copy the list and refer to it whenever you're stocking up on office supplies. You could even keep a laminated copy near your supply area (or closet) and circle in wax pencil or dry erase marker, the items you need to buy on your next trip to the store or when you order supplies on-line. Or, keep the list on your computer and update and print it as needed.

Basic Home Office Supplies

One-time purchases:

- Business card holder (if contact information is not stored electronically).
- Calculator (if you don't use the one in your computer).
- Check endorsement stamp.
- Clear boxes (shoe-box size and smaller) to hold office supplies.
- Computer disk or CD holders.
- Daily planner (paper-based or handheld if not computerized).
- Date stamp (if you want to track when information arrives).
- Drawer dividers (silverware trays work too).
- Hanging file frames for file cabinet (if not built in).
- Letter opener

- Stapler
- Staple remover
- Paper cutter
- Scissors
- Surge protector(s)
- Postal scale (may be leased—necessity depends upon how often you go to the post office).
- Clear tape dispenser
- Ruler
- Three-hole punch
- Uninterrupted power supply (UPS)
- Vertical (or desktop) file holder
- Wastebasket with shredder

Items you'll need to replenish:

- Address labels
- Business cards (yours, imprinted)
- Clear tape
- Computer disks (including Zip disks) and CDs
- Copy/printer paper (white, 20lb., 8 1/2" x 11")
- Correction fluid (white, plus color to match letterhead).
- Fax cartridges
- Fax paper (if not using plain-paper fax).
- Hanging file folders (plus clear and colored plastic tabs and inserts).
- Highlighter markers
- Three-ring binders
- Manila file folders
- Labels for file folders
- Legal pads

- Mailing labels
- Manila envelopes (9" x 12" and 10" x 13")
- Note-size stationery (imprinted paper and envelopes).
- Overnight-delivery packing supplies (envelopes and labels).
- Paper clips
- Pencils
- Pens
- Printer cartridges
- Rubber bands
- Stamps
- Staples
- Stationery (imprinted letterhead, plain second sheets, imprinted envelopes).
- Sticky notes

Shelves

A closet within a spare bedroom, den, or basement home office is a valuable asset, but a home office without a closet makes office-supply, reference-material, and product storage a challenge. Bookcases can hold reference books and computer and other electronic documentation, and in some cases, serve as a divider between two rooms being used for different purposes. For example, a home office within a loft space could be separated from a den with floor-to-ceiling bookcases. Hang pictures on the back of the bookcase to continue the illusion of a wall, or place the bookcases back to back.

If you don't want to buy more furniture, you can opt to line your walls with shelves. These may cost you less but require more work on your end to install. With a bookcase, you may only need to put a few pieces together and you're in business. To properly install shelves on your walls, you must first measure your walls and decide how much of them you want your shelves to take up. Then, you have to mark your walls with various shelf heights, taking into account that each shelf needs to be supported by at least two braces. The braces need to be screwed into the studs in the walls—otherwise your shelves will soon come crashing down. Also, you should not start nailing anything in until you've used a level to make sure your shelves are straight. You may want to call in a professional to take care of these headaches for you.

Making the Most of Closet Space

Time-wise, it's easier to place bookcases or metal shelving (often used in garages) inside a closet to store supplies and materials, but space-wise, you'll be wasting valuable space above, below, and beside where these pieces are stored. Your best bet is to custom build shelves within a closet so even if your office space is limited, you

Below left When bookcase space is limited, add shelves above the desk. Complete the look by painting the shelves to match the desk. Less frequently used items are stored out of the way on the highest shelf, yet remain visible.

Below right Converting a coat closet into a supply closet provides storage for supplies and reference materials, with space to tuck a rolling supply cart below when not in use. With the door removed and the storage closet located adjacent to the front door, keeping the closet organized is a must.

can avoid a cluttered look by tucking away office supplies and equipment on your closet shelves.

The standard height between shelves is 12 inches (30.48 cm), but you should consider the items you'll be storing in the closet while you're designing it. You may want to store extra large books or even equipment that you don't use very often. By designing the inside of your closet to meet your needs, you will be able to store the items to which you need frequent access, and will make use of every square inch of the closet. If you're not particularly handy and don't want to spend money on hiring a professional, look into the closet organizers available in most home and housewares stores. This wire shelving can be installed quickly and easily by just about anyone.

Don't forget about your closet doors. If you have a standard door or doors on your closet, attach a wire holder or purchase an over-the-door holder for supplies, reference materials, and anything else that you need to access regularly. Always place the items you use often within sight and reach. Anything you use less frequently should be stored on higher shelves or on the floor of your closet.

Furniture for Storage

Old dressers, buffets, and armoires are ideal for storing supplies: They can hold a wealth of supplies hidden from view, and if the piece in question is an antique or simply a really stylish

one, it can serve as the focal point in the décor of your office. Use drawer dividers as much as possible to keep items separated and easy to find. Clear shoe-box size (or smaller) containers work well on behind-the-door shelves and within drawers to keep items grouped by type of item. If your supplies will be stored in view, use clearly labeled baskets, metal holders, or colorful shoe boxes. If you're lucky enough to have a great old armoire, think about the countless ways you could adapt it. Add shelves, and you've got a great space for storing just about anything. Install a flip-down desktop, and you've got an all-in-one workspace that can be hidden away when you close up shop at the end of your workday.

Office Essentials

Okay, so you've got your space set up exactly the way you want it: you've purchased or built the perfect workstation(s), you've decorated the room to motivate and soothe you at the same time, and you've incorporated a grand storage system to keep everything in its proper place. So what's next? Well, it's time to stock up and put those storage units to good use.

When you worked in a corporate setting, the supply closet probably resembled the local office-supply store. Whatever you needed, from pens to paper to staples, was only a few doors or cabinets away. On top of everything else, at-home workers

TIME-SAVER TIP

Stock up. Make room in your office for stamps, registered and certified mail receipts, and Priority and Express Mail forms as well as packaging in various sizes for the overnight delivery service you use. The same goes for banking supplies. Always have a supply of filled-out deposit slips on hand. You'll cut the time you spend in the bank or post office in half. Also keep a few of these supplies in your car so if you're on the road and need to send something off in a hurry, you'll be prepared.

have to be in charge of the supply closet and therefore have to plan ahead for their office-supply needs. If you have an upcoming deadline, you don't want to have to rush out in the middle of printing a document to buy another ream of paper. The best way to keep your office-supply cabinet stocked is to use a standard list. If you're opening a new home office, the one-time list on page 84 will serve your well. After your initial trip, use the maintenance list on page 84 to keep yourself on track.

Fortunately, you don't have to use the standard metal cabinets found in most corporate offices to store your supplies. Instead, use a credenza (add a shelf if it's wide open in the middle), your bookcase, or a two-door cabinet with shelves. Just when you think you don't have another inch to store supplies, look at your office closet doors. You can add an over-the-door holder with pockets to hold tape, staples, sticky-notes, and other often-used supplies, or hang a clear shoe holder with pockets on the inside of the door.

How can you have a well-stocked office without having your office resemble an office-supply store? The key is to buy only what you need and to logically store these items near the place you will use them and make the best use of your storage space.

Above Wooden file drawers can hold more than files and serve as extra storage surfaces. Supplies stored in drawers are easier to organize and find when placed inside clear shoe boxes or plastic holders. The key to keeping the storage system organized is to label the outside of the drawers.

You can further divide the space by using different textures and colors in the décor to separate different functions. For example, you might put down a small section of vinyl or wood flooring in the section of your family room devoted to your office, while the rest of the room is covered in wall-to-wall carpeting. A different, but complementary, shade of paint can make the office seem even more removed from the rest of the room.

Closing Up Shop

Using furniture or decorating tricks to hide your office when you're not working will make it easier to make the break from work when you need to. If a room divider will be too cumbersome, why not hang some roll-down shades that hang from ceiling to floor? Roll them up when you're working, and when you're done for the day, unroll them to tuck your office comfortably out of sight—and out of mind.

Another way to tuck your office away is by investing in furniture that disguises it. A modern computer workstation might be hard to ignore in a formal living room, but an antique desk could look perfectly at home. If you inherited some of your grandmother's old furniture, including a sideboard, dresser, or hutch, put it to work. Depending on the piece, you may find an antique is the perfect place to store supplies and files. Just think creatively. For example, an Art Deco bar can serve as a functional office-supply cabinet. Its two side cabinets can hold extra file folders, a two-door cabinet in the middle can store extra printer cartridges, pens, and pencils, and the three drawers below can house additional supplies. A piece that is functional and attractive is invaluable.

Perhaps the most adaptable of all computer workstations, an armoire unit can hold just about everything you need when you need it, and hide it all when you don't. Computers and other business equipment fill armoires in various

sizes, styles, and materials. These pieces blend in with the rest of a home, offer privacy if the room doubles as a guest room, and can house most if not all of a professional's equipment. Unlike a computer workstation, an armoire can fit into the décor of most any room. You can purchase a new one—they're available in a variety of styles and price ranges—or retrofit an existing one with shelves and a drop-leaf desk.

The Mobile Office

If you'll occasionally need to revert your space back to its original purpose—for Thanksgiving dinner, for example—consider putting your entire workstation on wheels. Fitted with heavy-duty wheels, a sturdy desk that holds all your computer components can be simply unplugged and rolled into a closet or out to the garage when you're expecting company. Rolling files offer similar advantages, and come in a variety of sizes and configurations, and are available in virtually every material from exotic hardwoods to inexpensive plastic.

Client-Friendly Office Space

Creating professional space within a real-life home is always a challenge. After all, you started working from home to get out of the corporate world, but in order to get work, you need to appear as professional as possible. Laundry baskets overflowing with dirty clothes, toys scattered about, and newspapers that haven't quite made it to the recycling bin are not only unprofessional, they're a business risk. After all, you need to be twice as professional as your corporate competitors in order to convince your clients that you mean business.

If you'll be entertaining clients in your home office on a regular basis, try to create a separate entrance to your home office to avoid having your clients walk through your home. If there is no logical place to put another entrance, you will have to keep on top of your housework. Before a client enters your home, close the doors to any rooms you don't want clients to see. Create space within or near your home

TIME-SAVER TIP

There is no designated start or end time for your work schedule at home. Take advantage of not having to "punch in" by working a schedule that best suits you. Most businesses open at 9:00 AM—if you're a morning person, why not get to work at 7:00 and enjoy a couple hours' peace before the phone starts ringing and the rest of the work world comes to life. If you're more of a night owl, once you've fed the kids and watched your nightly TV shows, sit down at your desk and prepare for the morning. You'll be surprised how much you can get done in the off hours.

office for client and staff meetings. To visually separate that space from the rest of the office, light it with accent or decorative lighting, such as spot lights, track lights, torchieres, or concealed lighting. Use accent lighting to create a more professional atmosphere in your home office, enhance architectural features or furnishings, and bring attention to artwork, academic honors, or professional awards.

If you don't have room within your home office to accommodate client meetings, make your dining room do double duty as a conference room. Improve the privacy of the space by adding French doors, a Japanese screen, or a half-wall made out of glass blocks. A nearby buffet can store legal pads, pens and pencils, and even a small whiteboard—the corporate version of a chalkboard—for illustrating key points during a meeting. Rather than having to run back and forth to the kitchen during meetings, set up a coffee station: invest in a few thermal carafes and water pitchers, an attractive ice bucket, or perhaps a dorm-sized refrigerator. Don't forget to have a supply of innocuous coffee cups available: your fine china will seem pretentious, disposable cups look tacky and tend to spill, and you'll lose any sense of professionalism if you serve your next big client a hot beverage in your favorite World's Greatest Mom coffee mug.

Thinking About Décor

The traditional spare-bedroom home office furnished and accessorized to match the rest of the home has been replaced with custom-designed home offices and attractive, modern offices that entice a home office professional to go to work.

Remember, a beautifully designed office is not necessarily a functional one. Decked out with fine furnishing, huge bowls of fresh flowers, and perfect objects d'art stylishly placed, an office space might resemble a scene from the latest issue of *House Beautiful,* but may have little function aside from being a showcase. Offices are hard-working rooms: they require furniture that is practical and well designed. Desks must be sturdy, chairs must be comfortable, shelving units must be adaptable and expandable. Like kitchens and baths, form must follow function. But you don't have to sacrifice style and design for order and practicality. The two can work hand in hand.

Read architecture and interior design magazines for inspiration, and think about how you are going to use your office (for writing, meetings, bookkeeping). Then design your office to meet those functions, and infuse it with plenty of design elements that appeal to your personal sense of style. The beauty of a home office is that it can reflect both your personality and the way

KEEPING TIDY

If you'll be meeting with clients at home, remember you've got to keep more than just your work area tidy. Make sure that any rooms your client has to pass through are not only neat and clean but also attractive and orderly. Don't forget the bathroom: keep it pristine and devoid of personal items—from hairbrushes to prescription medicines—whenever you're expecting clients. If you receive clients frequently, consider enlisting a cleaning service once a week to keep clutter and dust at bay in these areas.

Below **A primarily white home office has a clean, simple look without seeming sterile. The adjacent sitting room is ideal for client meetings or problem-solving sessions.**

you work—after all, those two elements of your personality are intrinsically related.

Working from home versus in a corporate office means you use fabrics in the colors and patterns you choose, without having to seek approval from others. If pastels make you happy, paint your office a soft yellow, sky blue, or pale pink for a soothing effect. If you prefer a more traditional look, patterned wallpaper in burgundy, hunter green, and navy blue will give you the look you want. Think about the way you work best, and tailor your arrangement to capitalize on your habits. Do you enjoy working early in the morning when the light hits your office just right? Then make sure you arrange your office to capture every ray of sunlight, and use soft, light-filtering window treatments and a bright, light-reflecting hardwood floor. If you find a formal atmosphere makes you feel more pro-fessional and motivated, invest in a beauti-

ful desk and make your space as businesslike as possible.

Your home office is a place where you can express your personality. If you enjoy gardening, flowered wallpaper and plants can make working in your home office a pleasure. If you're a sports fanatic, line the walls with framed sports photos or accent bookcases with exciting sports memorabilia. If you're a big fan of The Three Stooges, a home office is the ideal (and with regard to a spouse, possibly the only) place to hang your favorite framed posters of America's Knuckleheads.

The choice is yours. If you feel more comfortable working in a traditional, corporate office space, design your office accordingly. If, however, you fare better in an interesting and inspiring environment, let your creativity flow and transform your functional space into a home office heaven.

Above The white
cabinets, bright
fabrics, and over-
stuffed furniture make
this office inviting and
irresistible. The
glass-front cabinets
give the office an
open feeling and lend
more visual interest
than solid cabinets.
The oversized ottoman
on wheels is more
versatile than an
ordinary coffee table.

BEFORE you set up filing systems within your file cabinet, get to know these filing secrets.

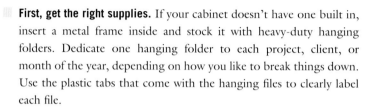

Filing Secrets

First, get the right supplies. If your cabinet doesn't have one built in, insert a metal frame inside and stock it with heavy-duty hanging folders. Dedicate one hanging folder to each project, client, or month of the year, depending on how you like to break things down. Use the plastic tabs that come with the hanging files to clearly label each file.

Use manila file folders as subdividers within each hanging file. You'll keep your file folders manageable by keeping them half an inch thick (about fifty sheets) or less. When they get thicker than that, divide the file folder into subcategories.

Files are only useful if you can find them when you need them. Keep track of your files by creating an index that lists all of your hanging and manila folders. This reduces the chance of duplicating files. Keep the index on your computer so you can update it when necessary.

Before you file a piece of paper, write in the top right-hand corner the name of the file where it belongs. This not only makes filing easier for you, but for anyone you choose to delegate the task to. Another option is to highlight a key word that corresponds to an existing file. Again, refer to your index: you'll save yourself the headache of creating new files unnecessarily because you weren't certain if a duplicate file already existed.

The best way to see the labels on your hanging folders is to stagger the tabs. You may like to place them all in a row, but unless your hanging folders are full, it will be difficult for you to see the rest of the tabs. Stagger the manila folders within each hanging folder so that you can see each one easily.

If you're motivated by color assign colors to different topics. Consider color-coding to make retrieval and replacement of the files simple. For example, make your financial files green and your client files red. Or, assign a different color to each project.

Most importantly, remember to purge your files regularly to eliminate paper.

Left Each inch of this home office is used for storage or as a work surface. Magazines stored in holders are accessible, yet don't block the main workflow. The wood-planked desk with desktop file holders keep active papers within reach.

Keeping Both Houses in Order

An untidy, disorganized office is a non-functional office. Not only do mounds of paper and scattered notes distract you from your work, they also distract you from your home life when you're not working. Just as it's important to keep the laundry out of the office, it's also imperative to keep your work from spilling out into your home.

Create systems for keeping track of meetings, phone calls, bills, and projects while keeping paper under control. The following tips will not only help you streamline the flow of paper in and out of your office, they'll also help you get and stay organized and save a few trees in the process.

FINISHING TOUCHES

While potted plants on the desk and unusual sculptures on the credenza can dress up a home office and give it an interesting and unusual look, these accessories can get in the way of running an income-producing home office. While things of beauty can be inspiring and comforting in an office, they do not belong in the main workflow areas. Several potted plants spread throughout a home office near a window, on top of a bookcase, or near a reading nook can bring new life to a home office without getting in the way of your work. Similarly, the art you hang on the walls should be inspiring, but never distracting. Decorate your space to be soothing and comfortable, yet inspiring and professional.

Read the Mail Right Away

Nothing piles up like mail. If you can't deal with it right away, put it in one place, for example a stacking bin, and sort it at the end of the day. When sorting, take action on each piece of paper. Toss junk mail immediately (aside from the occasional catalog, unsolicited marketing mail is just plain clutter). Then move each piece of paper forward by putting it in a file; answering the correspondence (sometimes handwriting the response on the incoming letter will do); entering any action you need to take on your to-do list then filing the paper (or put it in a to-do bin after listing); or recycling it. Another option is to create separate files for mail that needs to be dealt with at once and for mail that can be revisited later in the week.

Have One Calendar for Both Your Personal and Professional Life

Here's one area where it's smart to mix business with pleasure. Not only will you be more coordinated in your scheduling—you'll never plan a business meeting when you have a soccer game to attend—you'll cut your paper usage in half. Or, invest in a personal digital assistant. You'll have your whole life coordinated electronically and you'll be living paper free!

Upgrade Your Rolodex—Electronically

Spend an afternoon inputting your Rolodex cards into your computer's address book database, and download it to your PDA, if you have one. Then, as soon as you get a new contact's information, make it a habit to put it right into this program. Be sure to back this file up on disk.

Keep Notes in a Notebook

Those tiny little notes you write to yourself on loose slips of paper or Post-it notes can never be found when you really need that information, so stop wasting the paper. Invest in a spiral-bound notebook—preferably one already divided into sections. Make one section your to-do list, one section your new ideas and inspirations list, and use one for goals—or whatever information is most important to you.

Use Both Sides of the Paper When Possible

If you're not making a presentation or sending a letter or business proposal, why not stock your printer or fax machine with "used" paper—and get some use out of the other side? When making copies, always copy on both sides of the paper. Not only will you be doing the planet a favor, you'll be cutting the space taken up in your filing cabinet by half.

Recycle

Use a small trash can (in a different color than your regular trash can) and use it for paper waste to be recycled.

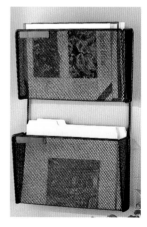

Keep in mind that while your business might get bigger, home office equipment is getting smaller by the day. Flat-screen monitors, tiny CPUs, and machines that function as scanners, printers, and copiers are already on the market and have become less expensive as they've become the status quo.

Offices with Room to Grow

One important and often overlooked aspect of home office design is the need to forecast the future of your business and the way that it will affect your space requirements. When designing a home, we often think about making room for children or even for our parents but rarely give the same consideration to adding employees to our home-based business. The advantage of a home office is that once you outgrow it, you can either expand it through remodeling or simply moving to another room in your home. If you know in advance that neither of these options is a possibility, do what you can in advance to choose the right space for your home office. Start by asking yourself a few questions when determining if your home office is expandable.

Could you expand the space you've chosen for a home office by knocking down an adjacent wall to create one large space? Don't get carried away: a large room may appear to be the perfect space, but too much space can become inefficient. Before you commit to any demolition projects, measure the entire space you want to use, lay out your office, and calculate how much extra space you'll have. The advantage of expanding your space is that obviously you'll have more space to work, while the disadvantage is that you'll lose a room in your home, which could affect its resale value.

Is there space outside your office (for example a porch or unused yard) that you could use for a remodeling project? An outside porch converted into an office will need to be insulated and may even need a separate heating and cooling unit, depending on the size. Converting the space will be cheaper than creating an office from the ground up, but when you design a new space, your only limitations are space and budget. With an existing space, you're limited to the existing structure.

The room you're currently using as a home office may have served you well when you started out, but now that you've outgrown it, there may be a better space. Could you switch rooms? For example, could you convert your larger den into a home office and turn your current office into a den? Take a close look at each room in your home and determine if it could be used differently.

Above **Flipping through files isn't for everyone (and neither is dropping papers out of files). Grab a three-hole punch and organize papers in binders complete with dividers inside and labels on the spine. When there's more shelf space available than drawer space, binders are the perfect alternative to files.**

The Working Office
Real Examples of Accessible Home Office Design, Furniture, and Storage Solutions

The options for creating attractive, functional home offices are endless. From a French country writer's cottage to a converted loft that houses a home-based Web-design firm, different spaces can be tailored to suit not only the work that happens in them but the personalities, tastes, and working styles of those who do the work.

This section features real-world examples of offices that work, beautifully. Investigating both the décor and the functional design, these pages will

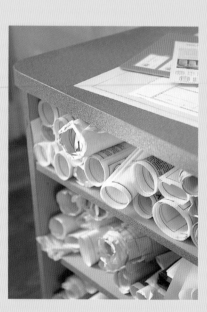

explain different options for outfitting and decorating your space, with real solutions for staying organized and maintaining a professional appearance at home. Remember that your space should be as professional as the corporate environment you left behind but as comfortable and personal as the home you've returned to.

Home Office Makeovers and Why They Work

IN MAGAZINES, BEAUTY MAKEOVER SUBJECTS undergo phenomenal transformations with the help of a hairstylist and makeup artist; indeed, it's hard to believe that the face featured in the "after" shot is even the same person who was pictured in the photograph labeled "before." The same is true of home office makeovers. When you are so closely tied to your home office, especially when you use it at least five days a week, you begin to block out worn carpets, scratched furniture, and a chair with no redeeming qualities left. Only when you step back and see your office through different eyes do you begin to see its design, structural, and functional flaws.

Multipurpose Makeover

Combining a guest room with a home office presents a few challenges, including how to fit a bed and workspace in one room without crowding either space. Used primarily as a guest room and secondarily as a part-time home office, this room combines both personal and business use seamlessly.

The narrow bridge on the desk provides an additional surface for frequently used items, leaving the desk free for spreading out papers. The drawers, complete with drawer dividers, store extra supplies including paper, pens, and letterhead.

The rolling file cart that stores supplies in the top drawer and files below, can be moved from the desk to the sofa wherever it's needed. When used as a guest room, the file cart is stored under the desk and the chair is placed between the desk and window to make extra room for the pullout sofa.

The magazines stored in the large yellow container (instead of on the desk) are moved to the sofa periodically and additional magazines are stored in the wicker basket in the corner.

Rather than occupy more of the room than necessary, the sofa bed is perfect for housing guests and ideal for reading when the guests have left. The sofa and overstuffed ottoman blend in well with the natural wood furniture, yet their interesting pattern adds dimension to the room.

The window shears let in just enough light during the day and provide privacy at night. The vase of calla lilies offers a nice touch without blocking the main workflow. With no small children around, the vase is safe from accidents.

The owner chose a bookcase with glass rather than wood doors to make it easy to locate reference materials and display her favorite books.

The traditional overhead light found in most older homes was replaced by a ceiling fan to improve circulation.

How the office could be improved: A few minor changes would improve the function of this office. The ceramic items within the bookcase could be moved to the top of the bookcase to make room for supplies stored in decorative baskets. An area rug in a color other than beige would reduce any echo, give the room a warmer feel and add to the decor. To add more light to the room, a light kit could be installed on the ceiling fan.

Miniature Makeover

Compact doesn't have to mean confining. Although this graphic designer's office is in a small space (see page 107), she has put every square foot to work. This contemporary office has design and function written all over it.

The ergonomically correct computer workstation has enough room to store her computer equipment and has plenty of space for office supplies. The storage shelf and four drawers hold supplies she uses regularly. Instead of traditional desk organizers, she has chosen a shiny pewter pencil holder and small boxes for paper clips and rubber bands. The articulating keyboard that also houses the mouse, closes out of sight when not in use. The CPU trolley keeps the CPU free of dust from the floor and pulls out easily for inserting disks or CDs.

Lighting isn't a problem with an extending lamp. Perched on the hutch, it's never in her way, yet accessible at all times.

She finally added a cushion (firmly attached to the back) to make her wooden chair (with five legs—a must for stability) more comfortable. The textured throw rug is thick enough to allow her to roll her chair around without gathering, and removes any hollow sounds from her office.

Right **Figure out your "work" personality before designing your office space. This graphic designer knows if she puts projects out of sight, she'll forget about them, so she keeps all work close at hand rather than in a closet.**

Instead of keeping client information in files, she stores most of her information on her computer. Still, she likes to keep some information in her files and regularly purges the papers she rarely refers to.

A big fan of using boxes for organizing, this graphic designer keeps card samples, reference materials and extra supplies in a nearby bookcase. Each box is clearly labeled to save time looking for the supplies she needs. An admitted lookout (see page 24), she stores designs for projects in progress near her desk, instead of in the closet.

The bulletin boards above her desk are for entertainment purposes only. She wouldn't dare keep to-do lists on them, for fear she would forget an assignment or lose an important phone number. She says that the mementos on the boards serve as a good distraction when she needs a break.

The table behind her computer workstation is used more than any other piece of furniture in her office. She likes to spread out designs, sketch new designs by hand before transferring them to her computer, and organize client presentation materials.

This office has served her better than her former office, a guest bedroom, in that she doesn't have to close up shop when guests arrive. Instead, she can keep her office as is and close the door at the end of the day.

How the office could be improved: There are only a few changes this designer should make. First, adding a torchiere in the corner (moving the standing tubes aside) would light her entire office. The more time she spends in front of her computer, the more important an adjustable chair will be. While the wooden chair may serve her well now, an ergonomically correct chair (see page 72) will offer more support and comfort.

Left This pharmaceutical representative's office reflects her design taste and style, and steers clear of a corporate look.

Prescribed Makeover

Can a home office be cozy with a brick wall in the mix? Sure, with the right furniture and accessories. This pharmaceutical representative's office with its black and cream color scheme is warm, interesting, and most important, functional.

She chose a multilevel computer workstation because of the design aspect as well as the open and closed storage capabilities. She admits to being a bouncing ball (see page 20), so she didn't want her files to be out in the open to distract her. Her desk file drawer, filled with clearly labeled hanging and manila file folders, holds her current files, while a four-drawer file cabinet in her closet holds older files. She keeps samples and promotional materials on shelves in her garage.

Not wanting to be reminded of her days in a corporate office, she uses nontraditional desk organizers, favoring clear jars for holding rubber bands and paper clips. She's gradually computerizing all of her contact names, but for now, when she receives a new business card, she stuffs it in a small tin tea box on her desk until she does her monthly entering.

The open shelves below her fax, hold extra supplies in a labeled black box and round metal containers. Her old desk—two file cabinets with a thick board across them—didn't have space for her CPU, so when shopping for a new computer workstation, a place for the CPU was near the top of her list.

Her favorite spot within the office is her overstuffed leather chair. Here, she catches up on the latest products she represents and plans her sales calls for the next day while at the same time relaxing. She hated to part with her old, worn recliner but wanted to update her entire office at the same time.

In her former position with another company, she was out of her office most of the time, so she didn't mind using one of her dining room chairs. When her responsibilities changed, so did her need for a more comfortable chair. The ergonomic curved backrest has alleviated any back pain she used to suffer from using her old chair.

Her allergies kept her from keeping the carpet that was originally in her office when she bought her home five years ago. She felt the carpet had served the previous owners well and opted to refinish the floor and add an area rug.

How the office could be improved? First, as she continues to spend more time in her office, in front of her computer, she'll find the need for a more ergonomically correct chair. Secondly, by moving the framed photos to the lower surface on the right-hand side of her computer workstation, she would have more room to spread out papers. Third, a wicker basket kept alongside her reading chair could hold a week's worth of newspapers before she took them to be recycled.

Going to Market

A marketing consultant with her own firm has many responsibilities. Although this professional's business keeps her out of her office on most days, she needs to make the best use of her time when she is in her office. Several elements come together to make this office highly efficient and organized. First, all of her equipment, with the exception of her computer, is stored along the back wall, above storage cabinets. Before organizing her space, she had to walk across the room to retrieve printed documents. Now, she simply rolls her chair over to the printer. Secondly, when working on large projects, she wheels her mobile storage cart next to her desk. The large task light mounted to the table shines light exactly where she needs it and swings out of the way when not being used. How could the office be further improved? There are two small changes she could make. The first is to add a bookcase to store the magazines stacked on the first row of shelves. Within the bookcase, she could store the magazines in individual holders labeled by title. The second is to label the boxes stacked on the second row of cabinets to make the contents easier to find.

Below With armoire closed, this home office is disguised as a guest room.

From Guest Room to Home Office

Sandra, a freelance writer, had always managed to meet deadlines from her makeshift garage office—a folding table and chair crammed into the corner. When her eldest son left home for college, Sandra seized the moment—and his attic bedroom. Torn between facing the reality of her son living on his own (at least part of the year), and her need to work in a "real office," she compromised by converting her son's bedroom into a partial home office/guest room. She knew he would come home during school breaks and wanted him to have a comfortable place to stay, but she couldn't bear to see a perfectly good room go to waste.

Sandra made clever use of the dormer by replacing the metal bed frame with a wooden platform with drawers below to store supplies. Between the light from the window adjacent to the bed and the light walls, the sleeping area eliminates a closed-in effect. The wooden bookshelf/headboard provides additional space for her favorite novels and a few decorative items.

To complete the conversion, Sandra opted for an armoire over a traditional desk or computer workstation for two reasons. First, she wanted the room to feel more like a bedroom than an office. When closed, the armoire fits in with the rest of the room and when open, she can get down to work. The second reason she chose an armoire was to keep visitors (even family) from using her computer or disturbing anything within her office when she wasn't at work.

All the equipment Sandra needs for writing, printing, faxing, and calling fits neatly into the armoire, with plenty of space for her to store reference materials and the supplies she uses often. The pullout table gives her room to research her next article or take a tea break. In addition to storing her current files in the lower file drawer, she uses a two-drawer cabinet in the closet. She likes the look of the hardwood floor, but to make the room feel warmer and to cushion the sound, she added an area rug.

Above When open,
the armoire trans-
forms the room into
a fully functional
home office.

Below This architect's plans are neatly stored and organized in open shelves.

Furnishing a Growing Home Office

As a successful architect, Jason knew that he had to apply the advice he had given to hundreds of clients to his own situation. It was time to expand his office as his business expanded. He had always dreamed of a "corner office" but a small desk in the corner of his bedroom wasn't what he had in mind.

Back when Jason started his architectural firm, the handful of clients he served and the paper they generated were manageable. After his little firm grew and he hired associates to handle the overflow, his small desk and file cabinet were no longer enough. He had to find another space for his home office.

Jason examined both his bedroom home office and the rest of his home looking for a better space. He settled on a spare bedroom that he had been using for storage. Most of the items in the spare bedroom needed to be tossed or donated anyway. With his mind set on turning the room into his home office, he had the motivation he needed to empty the room.

Jason's first step in converting his storage room into an office was to replace the carpet with a multicolored slate floor. Initially he was concerned about how much his office would echo without a rug, but decided that a small echo was better than using a plastic mat or catching the wheels of his chair on an area rug.

After measuring his available space, he said goodbye to his old desk and hello to a U-shaped arrangement made up of a lateral file, computer workstation and spacious desk. Every week, Jason meets with his associates—who work out of their respective homes—to review projects and share ideas. Everything, including his printer and phone, is readily accessible without devouring his workspace. The window on the left side of his desk allows plenty of light to stream in, yet his monitor is free from glare by being placed at an angle in the corner.

Wanting to make the most of the limited space in his office, he installed four shelves on either side of his desk to hold reference materials, books, and magazines. The large, clip-on desk lamp provides sufficient task lighting, while the track lights above the window provide additional light on his desk.

The photos tacked to the four bulletin boards mounted above his lateral file cabinet add a personal touch to Jason's office. He stores incoming mail in a wire mesh holder on the right-hand side of his desk.

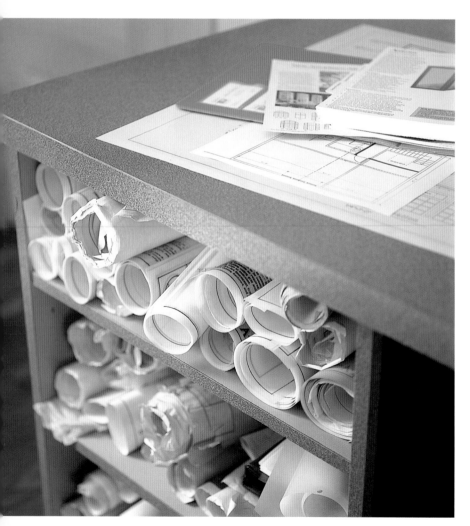

Above An architect's
U-shaped office
provides abundant file
storage, a large
surface for his
computer, and printer,
and a large desk for
reviewing plans and
meeting with clients
and associates.

Ordered Activity Design

A sales rep wears many hats, as does any home office professional, but with a boss to report to and clients demanding information at a moment's notice, organization is vital to this home office professional's survival.

After his wife quit her home-based business to work for her old employer, Mitchell took over her old office. While it served her needs, including an older Macintosh, Mitchell knew this new arrangement would be short lived. First of all, his boss told him that he would

make random visits to Mitchell's home office (fortunately he hadn't seen Mitchell's office yet) to review accounts and catch up on his territory's status. Aside from the outdated equipment, Mitchell needed file space and space to store supplies. His final bone of contention was the yellow walls. They had to go.

After painting the office white, Mitchell removed the heavy drapes, opting for a bare window. His wife had kept the drapes closed while she worked to avoid having to adjust her eyes between the window and monitor. With his new notebook computer and desk at a right angle to the window, he didn't need to worry about blocking out the sun.

All too happy to get rid of his wife's yellow lamp, he replaced it with a simple black-and-white extending desk lamp. He added a few containers for supplies and a magazine holder. Since his notebook computer occupies little space, he has plenty of desktop space to work.

Keeping reference books nearby, but not in the way, is important to Mitchell so he installed a long shelf high above his desk, but not so high that he can't reach what he needs.

The rolling file boxes below his desk are easily accessible and push out of the way when not in use. He keeps a two-drawer cabinet in a small closet within the room.

Mitchell's rolling desk chair is a far cry from the dining room chair his wife used to use. After he took out the old carpet, exposing the hardwood floors, he felt he had made a full transformation—from his wife's old setup, to one that fit his own work style and taste.

A Laundry Room Office Makeover

It's amazing how a small area can be converted into a functional, well-stocked home office. After the owner grew tired of working in the basement, this former laundry room (the washer and dryer were moved to the basement) became the prime spot for a new home office.

Below **Before**—this space was used as a laundry room, but the owner didn't want her office in the basement any longer.

Lesley turned her grandmother's antique desk into a functional computer workstation. She tried to use the lap drawer as a keyboard stand but felt more comfortable with the keyboard on top of her desk. (Most of the time she types with the keyboard in her lap anyway.)

Next she added a file cabinet—the perfect place for her fax and files. A firm believer in using colors for filing, her client files are red and her financial files are green. By opening the file drawer and taking a quick look at the tabs, she can see where each file is located.

She regulates the amount of light in her office by adjusting the cream-colored Roman shades, accented in black. The desk lamp with an adjustable arm directs the light to wherever she needs it most.

Lesley doesn't waste time looking for catalogs, reference materials, or supplies because they are organized in boxes of various sizes. Some of the boxes are labeled, while others aren't since she can tell what's inside by the type of container.

When looking for a new chair, she wanted function, style, and comfort. A cobalt blue chair fits all of her needs and adds color to her primarily beige office. She even has room in the corner for another chair that she uses for reading and brainstorming.

Lesley finds that she's more productive in her new office space although she's in a smaller space, yet she doesn't feel cramped. When she worked in the basement, the limited windows didn't make up for the dark and dingy feel of working below her home.

Above Use file cabinets with color-coded files for quick and easy research and retrieval. Clear storage containers allow you to see what is in each.

Working Home Offices

"BEAUTIFULLY DESIGNED" AND "FUNCTIONAL" do not have to be mutually exclusive terms when describing your home office. Many times, however, home office professionals sacrifice one for the other. To achieve an attractive, comfortable home office look, the right window treatments, flooring, and wall décor will play a large role. Also contributing to the overall look of your home office are your personal touches, from family photographs to reminders of favorite vacations. There are no hard-and-fast rules to follow when it comes to having a home office, except for the IRS requirement that only

business-related items may be stored in your home office, and only business-related functions may be performed in that space.

Break out of the traditional office mold and replace your beat-up metal file cabinet with an oak lateral file cabinet that will give you space on top to store your fax and desktop copier. Say goodbye to your back-breaking, pain-inducing, kitchen chair and replace it with an ergonom-ically correct office chair in a bright red or co-balt blue. The only boundaries you face in your home office are self-imposed. Create a space that is your own and you will use it often.

By reviewing the photos in this chapter, you will discover ways to improve your existing home office or be inspired to start over to design the home office you have always desired, yet assumed impossible to create.

Interior Designer's Office

An interior designer's home office doesn't have to be as complicated as her design plans. By using a simple file cabinet and L-shape set up, she has plenty of space to work while she's on the computer or talking with clients on the phone.

The natural wood used all throughout the office, including the beams on the ceiling, combined with the white walls and fireplace, give the office a light, airy feel. The picture leaning on the mantel rather than hung on the wall and the distressed side table make the office seem less formal and more inviting.

Not a true fan of ergonomics, this home office professional prefers to use a simple chair for her computer area and a stool at her drafting table. She spends more time out of her office than in, so she doesn't feel an ergonomically correct chair is absolutely necessary.

The large plant on the desk enhances the design of the office without hindering its function. It's set in an area that is used infrequently and serves as a divider between the computer area and drafting table.

The large and small throw rugs serve two functions. One is to add color to the office and the other is to cushion sound from the hardwood floors.

When clients occasionally visit her office—she normally meets with them in their homes—they use the couch and side table to examine plans.

The decorative items, with the exception of a small, framed photo and the large plant, are displayed off of prime desk real estate, leaving additional space to work. A collection of personal photos framed and hung between her two workstations adds a personal touch to the office.

Right **An L-shape desk set up next to a drafting board gives an interior designer plenty of surface area to review large drawings while on the phone or working at the computer.**

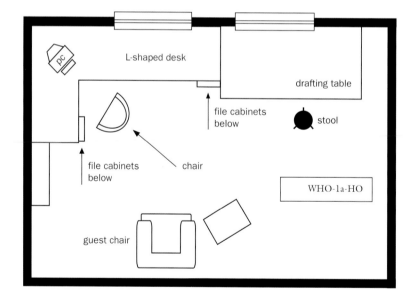

Web Designers' Office

Sometimes two is better than one and when two people share a home office, two spaces to work definitely are better than one.

The Web-designer couple who shares this home office used to work in a makeshift office in their garage. Their garage office worked well

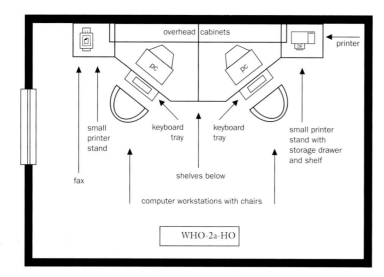

overhead cabinets

printer

pc

pc

small printer stand

keyboard tray

keyboard tray

small printer stand with storage drawer and shelf

fax

shelves below

computer workstations with chairs

WHO-2a-HO

until summers became warmer and the winters unbearable. They moved their younger son into his brother's room that had two twin beds (they often shared each others' rooms anyway) and created their own home office heaven in the younger son's room.

They often design sites together, so they wanted a setup that would allow them to view each others' screens quickly. In their other office, one partner was on one side of the garage and the other worked in the other corner. They found themselves going back and forth between both desks many times throughout the day, which was a waste of time and energy.

Although the computer workstations are next to each other, they provide plenty of room for each designer. Their printer is networked, eliminating the need for multiple printers.

Each designer has a small printer stand with a storage drawer and shelf. One stand houses the printer, while the other holds a fax machine. Instead of using traditional storage containers, they use metal boxes with slots in front for labels. They use notebooks rather than file folders to store most of their papers.

Rather than invest in a bookcase, they installed a combination of glass and solid-door cabinets. Inside, CDs and computer manuals are stored within reach, yet out of the way. (Frequently used CDs and disks are stored in between their monitors.) The spotlights below the cabinet, in addition to the adjustable work lamps on the workstations, offer a sufficient amount of lighting.

Their wooden desk chairs—the husband's choice—are surprisingly comfortable. At times they use a seat cushion, but for the most part find that the chairs meet their needs.

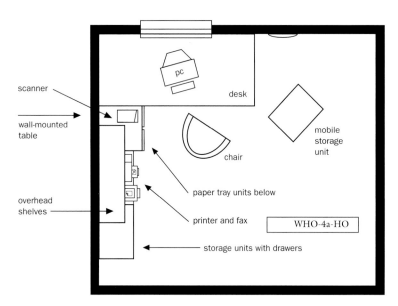

scanner

wall-mounted table

overhead shelves

pc

desk

chair

mobile storage unit

paper tray units below

printer and fax

WHO-4a-HO

storage units with drawers

Organized for Success

This office is a lesson in organization. Not only is everything in its place, the places are interesting and appealing.

Start with the shelves. Instead of traditional metal brackets, these wooden containers are held up by wooden brackets. The drawers, with a clever finger hole for easy opening, are deep enough to hold reams of paper inside and office supplies on top. All of the containers are square instead of round (a space saver) and clearly labeled to avoid confusion.

The storage unit below the shelves comfortably holds smaller items inside and the fax and printer on top. The opaque doors add an interesting design element and the wheels make reconfiguring this arrangement easy.

The paper tray unit with twelve slots for papers of various sizes and colors, eliminates the need for boring smoke-colored stacking trays. The wall-mounted table keeps even a large scanner within reach.

Originally, this home office professional didn't want to add window treatments but soon realized the need for blinds to regulate the amount of light coming into her office. She considered mounting a keyboard drawer to her desk but felt more comfortable with the keyboard on top.

She wasn't sure if she would enjoy using a desk without drawers until she stumbled upon a clear molded plastic storage unit. She likes the combination of two drawers with two open spaces below, plus the wheels to move it where she needs it.

The large steel hanging lamp offers the right amount of light on the left-hand side of her office, while the task light showers her workspace with light.

Livening up her office was her last challenge. She likes a natural wood look so instead of going with traditional black accents, she chose a splash of red on her chair and area rug. The potted plant provides additional color without cluttering her desk.

Writer's Office

An office that occupies only a small amount of space can be as effective as an office that fills an entire basement. It's all in the placement of supplies, materials, and equipment.

This home had only one space available for a home office—a corner of the den. Shelving was less of a challenge than work space. Instead of abandoning the idea of using this den as a home office, this writer made the best use of the available space.

She started with the drawers below the counter. She removed all of her personal items including old scrapbooks, cards from friends and relatives, and games her kids used years ago. She replaced those items with research materials stored in notebooks and the traditional dictionary, thesaurus, and style reference books.

The writer created a lighting plan that helped to make this corner into a hard-working home office. Even in this very small space, she was able to balance task lighting with general lighting to create a comfortable work area. Recessed downlights focus light on the main areas of activity and display—the desktop, window seat, and shelves. A flexible desk lamp can be adjusted to shine light on the keyboard, not the computer screen, where it can cause glare. As for natural light, she chose to do without window coverings—she likes to see the stars at night—and doesn't have to worry about blocking the daylight.

While she doesn't want to clutter her entire desk with personal items, she likes to keep family photos and magazines nearby. She painted the den's walls with a stimulating yet soothing color scheme—deep red calmed by a cool beige. Built-ins made of light-colored wood (the desktop, drawers, window seat, and shelves) lighten the effect of the deep red walls. You can use movable furniture instead of built-in pieces to achieve the same effect.

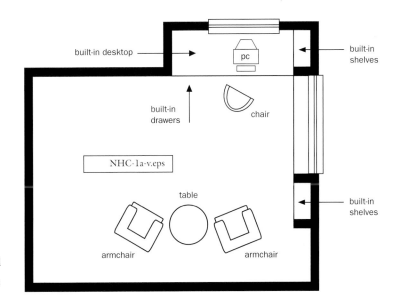

built-in desktop

built-in shelves

built-in drawers

chair

NHC-1a-v.eps

table

armchair

armchair

built-in shelves

Opposite **In a corner of a den, a freelance writer made the best use of limited space by storing research materials and books above her writing surface, in desk drawers and in the den's existing bookshelves.**

A literary agent's office, surrounded with windows and sliding doors, gives a full view of the large backyard and mature trees. The leather chair and ottoman create the perfect spot for reviewing manuscripts.

Literary Agent's Office

An office with natural wood and nature nearby isn't for everyone, but for those looking for a calm, peaceful setting, this office is ideal.

A literary agent's office can be traditional, or it can embody a more free-flowing atmosphere. After all, being bogged down with author submissions all day can be less than exciting.

This agent's office arrangement—a simple wooden desk—is large enough to spread out papers, read manuscripts, and review contracts without occupying too much desk space. Her monitor sits near the back of her desk while her wireless keyboard stays on the desk or is stored in the lap drawer. This new office is a big change from her former office, a leased space in an office building. After tiring of the long commute and rising overhead costs, she decided to move home.

The wall-to-wall built-in bookcase and cabinets provide ample storage for books, magazines, and supplies. The three drawers in the middle of the built-in house her files. Her client files are organized using hanging and manila folders, and since she returns all rejected manuscripts, she doesn't have to worry about needing extra storage space.

When working on her computer, she closes the blinds behind the screen to block outside light, if only partially. Otherwise, she enjoys the spectacular view of her backyard.

Her ergonomically designed chair is a major improvement over the cheap swivel chair she once used. Although she spent more money on the chair than she had originally budgeted, the gradual disappearance of her neck and back pain convinced her that the extra cost was worthwhile. She not only likes the chair's unusual looks, she likes the way it feels.

The large leather chair and ottoman are her favorite part of the office. She prefers to review proposals while relaxing in the chair instead of sitting at her desk. The area rug in the center of her office provides color and minimizes echoing.

Advertising Executive's Office

A large, U-shaped arrangement feels right at home within a huge home office space. This setup won't work in every home office, but when space is unlimited, why not think big?

This advertising executive's home office resembles a corporate office, with a few soft touches. From the art on the wall to the interesting desk lamp, his office exudes warmth and professionalism at the same time.

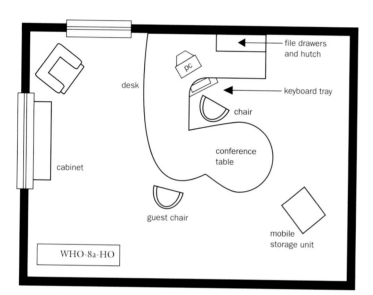

file drawers and hutch

desk

pc

keyboard tray

chair

conference table

cabinet

guest chair

mobile storage unit

WHO-8a-HO

This arrangement, a mixture of several sections, has limited drawer space for supplies, but plenty of filing space. The file cabinets on one end are color-coded by client and publisher. Instead of storing supplies below, he stores supplies in the windowed cabinets of the hutch. An admitted perfectionist (see page 24), this home office professional works better without clutter. On busy days, files cover his desk (neatly aligned however), but by the end of the day, everything is put away.

The articulating keyboard and ergonomically correct chair make computer work comfortable and a pleasure. Whether he's thinking of a new approach one of his clients should take or reviewing his own marketing plans, this setup leaves him with room to spread out his papers and make long-term plans.

He uses the conference table on one end for meetings with his two employees and the two subcontractors who work from their own home offices. The pencil-look table legs add a personal touch to the office and help him avoid a true corporate look.

His favorite area of the office is the reading corner. The nearby cabinet holds the books he plans to read one day and past issues of business publications.

He thought he would miss renting outside space as he had done for the past fifteen years, but after furnishing his office to complement his working style, he wonders why he hadn't moved home years ago.

Resource List

The sources listed in this section provide everything from furniture to lighting to equipment and software. Contact these companies by phone or via the Internet to receive more information about their products or services.

Furniture

Computer Furniture Direct

(800) 555-6126

www.cf-direct.com

Home office furniture isn't difficult to find. Finding furniture to accommodate a monitor, CPU, printer, fax, and other technology have-to-haves is a bigger challenge. This site offers solid oak and veneer furniture that has been designed specifically for home office use. Several steps up from RTA (ready to assemble) furniture, Computer Furniture Direct offers sturdy pieces that are delivered assembled, which means no Bob Vila-like skills needed.

Crate & Barrel

(888) 249-4158

www.crateandbarrel.com

Known more for its household accessories, extensive cooking supplies, and decorative place settings than its home office furniture, Crate & Barrel has jumped into the home office market with both feet. Ranging from hardwood to pine desks, bookcases and armoires, and traditional to eclectic pieces, these items are designed for longevity. On occasion you'll find their furniture on sale, which is a nice break for their pricier items.

Design Within Reach

www.designwithinreach.com

(800) 944-2233

If you're looking for traditional, run-of-the-mill furniture, this site may serve only to entertain you with its unusual designs. If you want cutting-edge, non-traditional furniture, this site is worth a look. Touted as a source that "provides easy access to well-designed furniture, frequently found only in designer showrooms," Design Within Reach has a long list of designers whose furniture they sell. Their primary customers are designers, but their products are available to the general public as well.

Ethan Allen

Ethan Allen Drive

P.O. Box 1966

Danbury, CT 06813-1966

(800) 228-9229

Ethan Allen used to be known for its all-traditional, American colonial furniture. The traditional pieces are still available, but today are overshadowed by more modern, functional furniture. Their updated line of higher-end home office furniture isn't designed for the discount-minded, but anything purchased from this store is designed to last.

Furnitureonline.com

(800) 407-8273

www.furnitureonline.com

This site offers computer workstations, home office centers (armoires), seating, and lighting. It's easy to navigate and the prices are comparable to office supply superstores and mid-priced furniture catalogs.

Full Upright Position

1200 NW Everett

Portland, Oregon 97209

(800) 431-5134

www.fulluprightposition.com

"The modern furniture company" is the perfect description for this company. Whether you want an oddly shaped desk or chairs that are guaranteed icebreakers for home office client meetings, this catalog has it. The "you get what you pay for" theory applies here—it isn't cheap, but creativity costs.

Haworth, Inc.

One Haworth Center

Holland, MI 49423

(616) 393-3000

www.haworth.com

All of their desks and storage units are available through a dealer network. A dealer locator service, complete with detailed maps, is available on their site.

Herman Miller for the Home

www.hmhome.com

Herman Miller, Inc., an international firm that makes and sells commercial and residential furniture, offers a variety of home office furniture, storage, and accessories. If you're ready for a new home office but don't know where to start, the Herman Miller "room planner" enables you to create a custom-made, "virtual" room that's formatted to the dimensions of your home. You can design your office with over 150 pieces of Herman Miller furniture, various windows and doors, and even pets scaled to size (although you'll have to buy or adopt those somewhere else).

Hold Everything

Mail Order Department
P.O. Box 7807
San Francisco. CA 94120-7807
(800) 421-2264
www.holdeverything.com

Stylish and functional furniture made of light and dark solid wood including maple and pine fill the Hold Everything catalog. They offer an interesting selection of desks, computer workstations, armoires, storage, and accessories.

IKEA

(800) 434-4532 to place orders and for store locations
(410) 931-8940 East Coast
(818) 912-1199 West Coast

Ikea has a wide selection of cleverly designed furniture available in wood, steel, and glass. Some of the units are on strong casters (ideal for a guest room doubling as a home office) and their desk accessories go beyond the typical smoke gray stacking trays and pencil holders. Call or visit their website for a catalog and store locations.

Knoll

1235 Water Street
East Greenville, PE 18041
(800) 445-5045
www.knoll.com

Desks, storage, chairs, lighting and accessories. Knoll carries a variety of stylish, yet functional furniture for corporate and home office use. While some of their designs are untraditional, others are designed with ergonomics in mind.

Levenger

420 S. Congress Avenue
Delray Beach, FL 33445-4696
(800) 544-0880
www.levenger.com

Self-described as "tools for serious readers," Levenger offers a few high-end pieces of home office furniture, plus accessories. Their Euro Desk system is made of solid and veneered American neutral or dark cherry. Levenger trades bargains for quality and style. (Products are available online, too.)

Lizell

P.O. Box 308
Routes 309 & 463
Montgomeryville, PA 18936
(800) 718-8808
www.lizell.com

Cutting edge, high-quality products, including furniture, fill the Lizell catalog. Some of the well-designed pieces are made with cherry veneers and solids and come in various configurations. They offer plush leather chairs, traditional wooden rolling desk

chairs and higher-end, ergonomically correct chairs. Their barrister bookcases with glass or wood fronts are the right size for most home offices. Bargain hunters will have to search elsewhere, but quality, design, and style-hunters will feel right at home. (Products are available online, too.)

L.L. Bean

Freeport, ME 04033-0001
(800) 544-0880
www.llbean.com

Traditional, functional, and sturdy could be used to describe L.L. Bean's clothing as well as its home office furniture. Their computer workstations, fold-down desks, and bookcases in oak and country pine are sturdy and practical.

Office Depot

(888) GO-DEPOT
www.officedepot.com

Between trips to the office supply store for supplies, equipment, or desk accessories, you've probably noticed an entire section of the store dedicated to furniture. Mostly all furniture available at office supply superstores is ready to assemble (RTA). For a small fee, you can hire someone to assemble your new furniture at your home office. Sales associates generally are knowledgeable about the furniture, but if not, there is plenty of literature available on each desk to answer most questions. You can purchase items online, via their catalog, or in-store.

Office Furniture USA

Officefurniture-usa.com
(877) FIND-OFUSA (346-3638)

Available both online and through their dealer network, Office Furniture USA offers a complete line of office furniture at reasonable prices. They work directly with manufacturers and office furniture dealers to furnish home and corporate offices. To alleviate a common problem with deliveries, they formed their own trucking company to ensure fast delivery. They claim to have thousands of items available on their online catalog, and another two million through special order. Their showrooms are laid out as mini-offices to give a true feel of how a setup would look in a home office. They have an online dealer locator or call the toll free number for a dealer in your area.

Office Max

www.officemax.com
(800) 788-8080

As with Office Depot, Office Max offers a complete line of home office furniture, lighting, and electronic equipment. It's mostly RTA and the time you'll save trying to figure out how to put together each section is worth the small assembly fee they charge. You can purchase items online, via their catalog or in their stores.

Organized Living
(800) 862-6556 (call for a retailer in your area)

As the name implies, you'll find virtually every organizing product on the market along with knowledgeable sales people who can solve most organizing problems. Almost one third of the store is filled with home office furniture that ranges from basic to more sophisticated. Their U-shaped and L-shaped units can be configured to fit most home offices.

Pottery Barn
Mail Order Department
P. O. Box 7044
San Francisco, CA 94120-7044
(800) 922-5507
www.potterybarn.com

While mainly a home furnishings store, they offer a small selection of desks and armoires with an eye on the past. While placing a board over two, two-drawer file cabinets used to be an inexpensive way to put together a home office workspace, Pottery Barn features a modified, more functional (and more expensive) version.

Reliable HomeOffice
P.O. Box 1502
Ottawa, IL 61350-9916
(800) 869-6000

Reliable HomeOffice fits somewhere between an office supply superstore and a high-end retailer. Some items, for example lamps, are reasonably priced, while the furniture is pricier than a superstore, but not as high as an expensive furniture store. Along with home office furniture, they offer storage units and accessories.

Spiegel, Inc.
P.O. Box 182555
Columbus, OH 43218-2555
(800) 345-4500

Only a small portion of the catalog is dedicated to home offices, with the rest dedicated to clothing and home accessories. However, there are a few computer workstations featured that are reasonably priced. They also sell storage pieces and accessories.

Stacks & Stacks
www.stacksandstacks.com

The focus of this site is organizing products, but they offer a small selection of computer workstations, desks, storage units, and file cabinets that are reasonably priced.

Staples
(800) 333-3330
www.staples.com

This office supply superstore offers much of the same products as others superstores with comparable prices. You can purchase items online, via their catalog, or in their stores.

Steelcase, Inc.
(888) STEELCASE (for dealer network)
www.steelcase.com

Whether you want freestanding desks, and files and storage cabinets, or various workstations to house multiple home office staff, Steelcase offers several solutions. Some of their lines utilize a wood and laminate system of freestanding furniture in traditional and non-traditional shapes and surfaces. While their site doesn't list furniture under "home office," their different lines can be adapted for the at-home worker. This site is chock-full of product information, workplace questions, answers and guidance, as well as products and dealer information.

Techline
500 South Division Street
Waunakee, WI 53597
(800) 356-8400
www.techlineusa.com

Techline manufacturers desk units, computer desks, shelving units, and storage. Many Eurway stores carry Techline products. Their 800 number or website can direct you to a Techline Studio or a retailer in your area.

Thomasville Home Furnishings
P.O. Box 339
Thomasville, NC 27361-0339
(800) 927-9202
www.thomasville.com

Known for its traditional furniture, Thomasville offers workstations, desks and computer armoires in cherry and oak finishes. Their 800 number or website will direct you to a retailer in your area.

Workbench
180 Pulaski Street
Bayonne, NJ 07002
(800) 736-0030
www.workbenchfurniture.com

They offer traditional and modern collections made with natural oak, maple, teak, or cherry veneers. Their reasonably priced furniture is designed with function in mind, but still qualifies as stylish. Call or visit their site for catalog and store locations.

Lighting
Luxo Corporation
36 Midland Avenue
Port Chester, New York 10573
(800) 222-5896
www.luxo.com

Features various lighting options including a large selection of task lighting. Call for store locations.

Walls and Windows

Hunter–Douglas
2 Park Way South
Upper Saddle River, NJ 07458
(800) 327–2030
All types of window treatments;
call for store locations.

smith+noble
(800) 560–0027
www.smithandnoble.com
All types of window treatments
from blinds to shutters to
cornices and valances. Call
or visit their site to request
a catalog.

Decoratetoday.com
(800) 575–8016
www.decoratetoday.com
They offer a complete selection
of wallpaper, blinds, custom-
framed art, rugs, lighting, and
home accents. There is also an
instant chat feature that lets you
talk in real time to one of their
decorating experts. Orders
taken online.

Storage and Organization

California Closets
(800) 873–4264
Customized, built-in systems
for home offices and storage
closets.

The Container Store
(800) 733–3532
Call or visit website for catalog
and store locations.

Fellowes Manufacturing Company
1789 Norwood Avenue
Itasca, Illinois 60143–1095 USA
Phone: 630.893.1600
www.fellowes.com
Makers of ergonomically correct
electronic accessories. Products
available at office supply stores.

Get Organized
(800) 803–9400
www.getorginc.com
Call for catalog.

Hold Everything
Mail Order Dept.
P.O. Box 7807
San Francisco, CA 94120–7807
(800) 421–2264
Call for catalog and store
locations.

Intrigo
350 Conejo Ridge Avenue
Thousand Oaks, CA 91361
Phone: (805) 494–1742
www.intrigo.com
Makers of the Lapstation.

Levenger
420 S. Congress Avenue
Delray Beach, FL 33445–4696
(800) 544–0880
www.levenger.com
Call or visit website for catalog.

Lillian Vernon Neat Ideas
Virginia Beach, VA 23479–0002
(800) 285–5555
Call for catalog.

The Mobile Office Outfitter
1046 Sepentine Lane #306
Pleasanton, CA 94566
(800) 426–3453
www.mobilgear.com
Call or visit website for catalog.

Organized Living
(800) 862–6556
(see listing under furniture)

Solutions
(800) 342–9988
www.solutionscatalog.com
Call or visit website for catalog.

Stacks & Stacks
www.stacksandstacks.com

Office Supplies

At Your Office
www.atyouroffice.com

Office Depot
(888)-GO-DEPOT
www.officedepot.com

Office Max
(800) 788–8080
www.officemax.com

Penny Wise Office Products
(800) 942–3311
www.penny-wise.com

Quill
(800) 982–3400
Quill Corporation
P.O. Box 94080
Palatine, IL 60094–4080
www.quillcorp.com

Reliable Office Supplies
1001 W. Van Buren Street
Chicago, IL 60607
(800) 735–4000
www.reliable.com

Staples
(800) 333–3330
www.staples.com

Equipment and Software

Egghead.com
c/o Direct Response
P.O. Box 185
Issaquah, WA 98027–0185
(800) 344–4323
www.egghead.com

MacConnection and PC Connection
Attn: Customer Service
450 Marlboro St.
Keene, NH 03431
(888) 213–0259
www.macconnection.com
www.pcconnection.com

MacMall
2555 West 190th Street
Torrance, CA 90504
(800) 552–8883
www.macmall.com

MicroWarehouse
1720 Oak Street
P.O. Box 3013
Lakewood, NJ 08701–5926
(800) 397–8508
www.warehouse.com

Photo Credits

Abode, 32 (right); 83; 89; 123

Russell Abraham/Courtesy of Design Within Reach, 72; 115

Peter Aprahamian/©Homes & Ideas/ IPC Syndication, 19

Peter Aprahamian/©Living Etc./IPC Syndication, 21

Graham Atkins-Hughes/Red Cover, 10 (right); 27; 47 (bottom right)

John Bell, 144

Dominic Blackmore/©Family Circle/IPC Syndication, 92

Courtesy of California Closets, 81; 121 (right)

Courtesy of Crate & Barrel, 55; 73; 87 (top left); 103 (right); 107; 108

Grey Crawford, 13, 14; 30; 34; 42 (top); 46; 59; 95; 99; 103 (left); 112; 113

Michael Dunne/Elizabeth Whiting & Associates, 93

Eulenberg/Picture Press, 43; 58 (top)

Courtesy of Fellowes Manufacturing Company, 79

©Freundin/Salomon, 100 (middle)

©Freundin/Spachmann, 135

Tria Giovan/Michael Foster Design, 97

Victoria Gomez/©Living Etc./IPC Syndication, 85 (right)

Ken Hayden/Red Cover, 36; 82

Winfried Heinze/Red Cover, 47 (left)

Andreas Hermann/Picture Press, 54

Courtesy of IKEA/www.ikea.com, 6-7; 10 (left); 11; 18; 40 (right); 47 (top); 50; 56; 57; 63 (right); 66; 68; 70; 71; 74; 76; 77; 88; 90; 98; 101; 102 (left); 103 (middle); 111; 120 (right); 125; 129

Tim Imrie/©Family Circle/IPC Syndication, 37, 41

Courtesy of Intrigo, 15

Lu Jeffrey/Elizabeth Whiting & Associates, 42 (bottom)

Syrial Jones/©Homes & Ideas/ IPC Syndication, 87 (right)

Tom Leighton/©Living Etc./IPC Syndication, 102 (middle); 117

Di Lewis/Elizabeth Whiting & Associates, 33

John Edward Linden, 45; 60; 133

©Lisa W & D, 85 (left)

©Living Etc./IPC Syndication, 126

Courtesy of Lizell, 69; 75 (top left); 75 (top right & middle); 120 (left); 137

Norenberg/Picture Press, 89

Reliable Home Office, 75 (bottom); 87 (bottom left); 100 (right)

Eric Roth 12 (left); 28; 62; 78; 84; 100 (left); 102 (right); 114

Courtesy of SALA Architects, 121 (left); 130

Tim Street-Porter, 31 (bottom); 39; 40 (left); 58 (bottom); 63 (left)

Thurmann/Picture Press, 64

Brian Vanden Brink/Axel Berg, Builder, 91

Brian Vanden Brink/Centerbrook Architects, 23; 32 (left)

Brian Vanden Brink/John Gillespie, Architect, 24;

Brian Vanden Brink/Winton Scott Architects, 61

Brian Vanden Brink/South Mountain Company, Builder, 16;

Wegner/Picture Press, 31 (top); 48; 53

Simon Whitmore/©Living Etc./IPC Syndication, 12 (right); 25; 116

Willig/Picture Press, 51; 96

Courtesy of Workbench, 104

Polly Wreford/©Homes & Gardens/ IPC Syndication, 118; 119

Index

About the Author

Lisa Kanarek is one of the nation's leading home office experts and the author of *Organizing Your Home Business, 101 Home Office Success Secrets*, and *Everything's Organized*. She is the founder of HomeOfficeLife.com, a firm that advises corporations and individuals on all aspects of working from home, including physical set-up, technology, productivity, and transitioning from a corporate office to a home office. Kanarek is a frequent speaker to Fortune 500 corporations, a regular contributor to national and international publications, and a former contributing editor for *Home Office Computing* magazine. Her clients include American Airlines, ABC, Avery, Fuji, Hallmark Cards, Johnson & Johnson, JC Penney, Lexmark, Microsoft, Office Depot, Sprint, Texas Instruments, and Volkswagen, among others.

Kanarek has been a guest on several national programs, including *Good Morning America*, CBS' *Up-to-the-Minute*, CNBC, American Public Radio, Public Radio's *Marketplace*, and Voice of America radio. Articles by and about Kanarek have appeared in hundreds of *publications, including The Wall Street Journal, The New York Times, Newsweek, Success, Money, Entrepreneur, Cosmopolitan, Home Office Computing, Working at Home, Working Woman, Marie Claire, Redbook* and *Nation's Business.*

Kanarek's weekly feature, Homework, airs nationally on the Public Television program, "Small Business School."

ALSO BY LISA KANAREK:

Organizing Your Home Business

101 Home Office Success Secrets

Everything's Organized